Structure & Speaking Practice
Fes

NATIONAL GEOGRAPHIC
LEARNING

Australia • Brazil • Mexico • Singapore • United Kingdom • United States

National Geographic Learning,
a Cengage Company

Structure & Speaking Practice, Fes

Becky Tarver Chase and Christien Lee

Publisher: Sherrise Roehr

Executive Editor: Laura LeDréan

Managing Editor: Jennifer Monaghan

Digital Implementation Manager,
Irene Boixareu

Senior Media Researcher: Leila Hishmeh

Director of Global Marketing: Ian Martin

Regional Sales and National Account
Manager: Andrew O'Shea

Content Project Manager: Ruth Moore

Senior Designer: Lisa Trager

Manufacturing Planner: Mary Beth
Hennebury

Composition: Lumina Datamatics

Student Edition: Structure & Speaking Practice, Fes
ISBN-13: 978-0-357-13799-4

National Geographic Learning
20 Channel Center Street
Boston, MA 02210
USA

Locate your local office at **international.cengage.com/region**

Visit National Geographic Learning online at **ELTNGL.com**
Visit our corporate website at **www.cengage.com**

Printed in China
Print Number: 02   Print Year: 2019

Photo credits

001 (c) ©Mark Henley/Panos, **002** (br) ©7-11 Corporate Communications, **002** (bc) Science History Images / Alamy Stock Photo, **002-003** (c) Bettmann/Getty Images, **003** (bl) Carl Clark / Alamy Stock Photo, **003** (br) Maksym Yemelyanov / Alamy Stock Photo, **004** (t) Kelly Cheng/Getty Images, **006** (t) ©GMB Akash/Panos, **011** (t) Jon Hicks/Getty Images, **012** (t) Bloomberg/Getty Images, **015** (t) Jeffrey Blackler / Alamy Stock Photo, **017** (b) Bloomberg/Getty Images, **019** (b) ZUMA Press, Inc. / Alamy Stock Photo, **021** (c) Suzi Eszterhas/Minden Pictures, **022-023** (c) ©Mark Moffett/Minden Pictures, **023** (br) DESIGN PICS INC/ National Geographic Creative, **023** (tr) ©Norbert Wu/Minden Pictures, **024** (t) JOHN EASTCOTT AND YVA MOMATIUK/National Geographic Creative, **024** (br) CengageLearning, Inc., **026** (t) ©Steve Winter/ National Geographic Creative, **029** (tl) Pixeljoy/Shutterstock.com, **029** (tr) STOCKTREK IMAGES/National Geographic Creative, **029** (cr) Justin Guariglia/National Geographic Image Collection, **029** (cl) STOCKTREK IMAGES/National Geographic Creative, **029** (bl) Tim Graham/Getty Images, **029** (br) Tim Graham/Getty Images, **031** (t) LU ZHI/National Geographic Creative, **032** (t) Kip Evans / Alamy Stock Photo, **032** (cr) Cengage Learning, Inc., **034** (bc) Christian Ziegler/ National Geographic, **036** (t) RAYMOND GEHMAN/National Geographic Creative, **038** (t) REZA/National Geographic Image Collection, **041** (c) ©Doug Gimesy, **042-043** (c) National Geographic Maps, **045** (tr) Cengage Learning, Inc., **045** (t) Bloomberg/Getty Images, **046** (cl) Mike Goldwater / Alamy Stock Photo, **046** (cr) CHRIS JOHNS/National Geographic Creative, **049** (t) Fernando Vazquez Miras/Getty Images, **050** (t) Olena Suvorova / Alamy Stock Photo, **052** (t) ©JR/ Redux, **055** (t) STANLEY MELTZOFF / SILVERFISH PRESS/National Geographic Creative, **057** (t) ©NASA/JPL-Caltech/ Univ. of Arizona, **059** (t) ©NASA/National Geographic Creative, **061** (t) ©Emotiv.

Scope and Sequence

Unit Title & Theme	Listenings & Video	ACADEMIC SKILLS Listening & Note Taking
1 **THE SCIENCE OF SHOPPING** *page 1* ACADEMIC TRACK: Behavioral Science	**Lesson A** An Interview about Consumer Behavior **VIDEO** The Decoy Effect **Lesson B** A Lecture about Consumer Behavior	• Recognizing a Speaker's Attitude • Reviewing Your Notes
2 **MOTHER NATURE** *page 21* ACADEMIC TRACK: Biology/Genetics	**Lesson A** A Panel about a Film Contest (with slide show) **VIDEO** Turtles under Threat **Lesson B** A Conversation on Campus	• Listening for Content Words • Noting Who Says What
3 **ON THE MOVE** *page 41* ACADEMIC TRACK: Sociology	**Lesson A** A Lecture about Migration (with slide show) **VIDEO** What Ellis Island Means Today **Lesson B** A Study Group Discussion	• Listening for the Order of Events • Noting Contrasting Ideas

Speaking & Presentation	Vocabulary	Grammar & Pronunciation	Critical Thinking
• Quoting Statistics • Asking Rhetorical Questions **Lesson Task** Designing a Store Layout **Final Task** Giving a Persuasive Presentation	Participial Adjectives	• Real and Unreal Conditionals • Question Intonation	**Focus** Recognizing Pros and Cons Predicting, Analyzing, Synthesizing, Reflecting, Personalizing, Making Inferences, Brainstorming
• Making Suggestions • Presenting with Others **Lesson Task** Discussing Conservation and Extinction **Final Task** Creating and Presenting a Proposal	Using Context Clues	• Adjective Clauses • Syllable Stress before Suffixes	**Focus** Deciding on Criteria Evaluating, Personalizing, Interpreting a Flowchart, Ranking, Synthesizing, Reflecting, Brainstorming, Organizing Information
• Expressing Probability • Expressing Your Opinion Strongly **Lesson Task** Discussing a Case Study **Final Task** Presenting a Viewpoint	Noticing Clues to Meaning	• *Enough* and *Too* • Linking	**Focus** Categorizing Information Predicting, Personalizing, Evaluating, Applying, Categorizing, Organizing Ideas

Independent Student Handbook, p. 61   Vocabulary Index, p. 76

THE SCIENCE OF SHOPPING

1

A woman looks at a window display of expensive jewelry in Shanghai, China.

ACADEMIC SKILLS

LISTENING Recognizing a Speaker's Attitude
Reviewing Your Notes
SPEAKING Quoting Statistics
Question Intonation
CRITICAL THINKING Recognizing Pros and Cons

THINK AND DISCUSS

1 The woman in the photo is window-shopping. Do you enjoy window-shopping? Why or why not?

2 Look at the title. What do you think this unit will be about?

EXPLORE THE THEME

Look at the photos and read the information. Then discuss the questions.

1. What information in the timeline surprises you?
2. Do you think shopping has changed positively over the years? Why or why not?
3. How do you think shopping might change in the future? Explain.

TWO CENTURIES OF SHOPPING

1890
Window Shopping
Shoppers look into the new glass display window of Marshall Field's department store in Chicago, Illinois, USA.

1796
Department Stores
The first department store, Harding, Howell and Company opens in London, U.K.

1893
Mail Order
Sears, Roebuck & Co. launches their first mail-order catalog, and continues filling orders until 1993.

1927

Convenience Stores
The first convenience store is opened in Texas, USA, by the Southland Ice Company and is later known as 7-11.

1956
Shopping Malls
Southdale Center, the first indoor shopping mall, opens in Minnesota, USA.

1962
Big Box Retail
The first Walmart store opens in Arkansas, USA, starting a trend of "big box" retailers, so called because they look like a big box.

1998

Vending Machines
Vending machines become very popular in Japan. In 1998, there are over 5.4 million machines there.

2010

Online Shopping
Online shopping and payments become more and more popular.

2017
Grab and Go
Amazon opens a new type of store that allows shoppers to pay electronically and leave the store without waiting in line to pay.

A Vocabulary

A farmers' market in Venice, Italy

A Look at the photo and discuss the questions in a small group.

1. What are some of the advantages and disadvantages of shopping at a market like the one in the photo?
2. Have you visited an outdoor market? If so, how was the experience? If not, would you like to shop at an outdoor market?
3. Do you think markets like this will still exist 50 years from now? Why or why not?

B 🎧 **Track 1** Listen to the words. Choose the best word to complete each definition. Then work with a partner to check your answers in a dictionary.

addictive	assume	bump	complex	purchase
alter	bargain	commercial	consumer	retail

1. _____ (adj) hard to understand or analyze

2. _____ (adj) related to business

3. _____ (adj) so enjoyable that one wants more of it

4. _____ (n) a person who buys goods or services for personal use

5. _____ (n) an item that one buys

6. _____ (n) something bought for a cheaper price than usual

7. _____ (n) the sale of goods or services directly to people

8. _____ (v) to believe without checking if it is true

9. _____ (v) to change

10. _____ (v) to hit with your body, especially by accident

Track 2 Complete these sentences with a word in **blue** from exercise B. Use the correct form of the word. Then listen and check your answers.

1. In the United States, many teenagers' first work experience is a job in _____ or in a restaurant.

2. Although the store only _____ the location of a few of the departments, many customers disliked the changes.

3. Ben had _____ that the store closed at six and was disappointed when he got there and found the door locked.

4. Customers frequently _____ into and knocked over the sign because of its inconvenient position.

5. Most people do not use a credit card when they make a very large _____ such as a new car.

6. During the end-of-year sale, hundreds of customers visited the department store hoping to find a great _____ or two.

7. Many _____ use their phones to check prices online before purchasing anything in a store.

8. In a survey of people who have bought items through online sites like eBay, some said they felt online shopping was so _____ that they couldn't stop doing it.

9. According to the plans, the new apartment building will have _____ space for offices, restaurants, and stores on the first floor.

10. The store's refund process was so _____ that many customers decided it was easier to keep an item than to return it.

D Work in a small group. First, choose five questions that you all find interesting. Then discuss them. Explain and support your reasons.

1. Do you assume that an item with a high price is always good quality? Explain.
2. In your view, which kinds of commercial buildings generally have the best design: stores, restaurants, or office buildings?
3. Would you agree that working in retail is good experience for a teenager?
4. In what ways do stores encourage consumers to buy things they do not really need?
5. Where do you shop to get the best bargains? What bargains have you found recently?
6. What is one past purchase that you regret buying? Explain.
7. When you have to study something complex, what study techniques do you find effective?
8. What do you say when you bump into someone? Are there times when an apology isn't necessary?
9. Who is most likely to make you alter your behavior and why: your family, your friends, or celebrities?
10. Would you agree that anything which is enjoyable could become addictive?

A Listening An Interview about Consumer Behavior

Shoppers ride on escalators in Bashundhara City, Dhaka's biggest shopping center, Bangladesh.

BEFORE LISTENING

A With a partner, make a list of things that consumers often do before, during, and after shopping, such as making a shopping list or trying items on. Then join with another pair and compare your lists.

WHILE LISTENING

CRITICAL THINKING:
PREDICTING

B 🎧 **Track 3** Work in a small group. Before listening to an interview with an environmental psychologist, discuss what you think her job involves. Then listen to the first part of the interview to check your answer.

LISTENING FOR
MAIN IDEAS

C 🎧 **Track 4** Listen to the whole interview. What do the speakers mainly discuss? Choose two answers.

a. how some stores try to influence their customers' behavior
b. what causes some people to become addicted to shopping
c. what factors might cause shoppers to take certain actions
d. which stores are more popular with shoppers than others
e. why shoppers are likely to touch or feel inexpensive items

LISTENING FOR
DETAILS

D 🎧 **Track 4** Listen again and take notes. Then check (✓) the five statements that match what the psychologist says.

1. _____ Consumers generally behave in complex ways when shopping.

2. _____ For shoppers, being bumped is sometimes bad, but sometimes OK.

3. _____ Shoes and shirts are common items that people buy online.

4. _____ Buying items at bargain prices can improve a person's mood.

5. _____ Shopping is a much more addictive activity than anything else.

6. _____ Stores are good at making people feel many positive emotions.

7. _____ Shopping when feeling bad can lead to increased spending.

8. _____ A number of different factors can affect how shoppers behave.

LISTENING SKILL Recognizing a Speaker's Attitude

🎧 **Track 5** Speakers often express an attitude—or how they feel—about certain things. Recognizing attitude can help you better understand a speaker's message. There are three main ways you can recognize a speaker's attitude:

1. A speaker may state what he or she is feeling directly.

   I'm really excited we're going shopping tomorrow. (excitement)

2. A speaker may express his or her attitude indirectly.

   It's too bad you can't come shopping tomorrow. (disappointment)

3. A speaker's intonation may help you recognize his or her attitude. For example, a falling intonation can indicate disappointment.

   She can't come shopping tomorrow.

E 🎧 **Track 6** Listen to four excerpts from the interview. Write the excerpt number next to the attitude of the speaker.

a. _____ confident   c. _____ thoughtful

b. _____ surprised   d. _____ uncertain

AFTER LISTENING

NOTE-TAKING SKILL Reviewing Your Notes

While you are listening and taking notes, it can be difficult to decide what the most important ideas are. This is why it is important to review your notes after you finish listening. First, add any information to make your notes clearer. Then, to review what you have learned, add a section at the bottom of your notes titled *Main ideas*. In that section, list three or four main ideas from the listening.

F Review your notes and make any additions to make them clearer. Then list three or four main ideas at the bottom of your notes. In a small group, compare your main ideas.

G Work in a small group. Discuss how it makes you feel that "stores are trying to alter" your behavior. Also discuss how you might shop differently now that you know this.

A Speaking

GRAMMAR FOR SPEAKING Real and Unreal Conditionals

The present real conditional describes something that is always or generally true. Notice that the two verbs in the sentence are both simple present.

*If I **buy** something on sale, I **feel** happy.*

The future real conditional describes a real or possible situation that has results in the future. Notice that the *if* clause is simple present while the result clause is future.

*If the price **drops**, I **will buy** it.*

The present unreal conditional describes something that is not true but can be imagined. Notice that the *if* clause is simple past and the result clause uses *would* + verb. Note that *were* is used for both singular and plural forms in the *if* clause of present unreal conditionals.

*If the price **were** cheaper, I **would purchase** it.*
*If I **had** money, I **would buy** a new laptop.*

A Work in a small group. Discuss these questions. Use conditionals in your answers.

1. If you need to buy clothes, where do you usually go shopping? Why?
2. If you have some free time next weekend, will you go to a mall? Why or why not?
3. If you could go anywhere on vacation, where would you go? Why?
4. What restaurant would you go to if you wanted to have a special celebration? Why?

CRITICAL THINKING:
ANALYZING

B Work with a partner. Look at the chart and complete the steps.

1. Imagine that you receive $10,000. How would you use the money? On what three things would you spend the money?
2. How are your ideas similar to or different from the information in the chart below?
3. Ask other students in the class what they would do with the money. Then share what you learned and create a chart showing the most popular ideas.

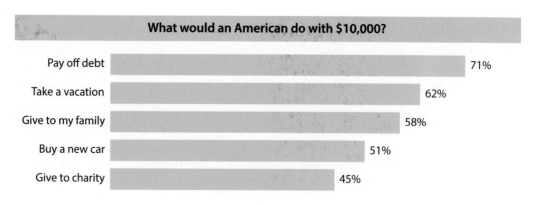

What would an American do with $10,000?

Pay off debt	71%
Take a vacation	62%
Give to my family	58%
Buy a new car	51%
Give to charity	45%

🎧 **Track 7** Questions in English typically have one of two common intonation patterns:

1. Rising intonation—the speaker's tone rises on the stressed syllable of the last content word. Rising intonation is common in *yes/no* questions.

   Is the store on the corner still open?

2. Falling intonation—the speaker's tone rises and then falls on the stressed syllable of the last content word. The content word depends on the focus of the question. Falling intonation is common in *wh–* questions.

   What did you buy yesterday? (focus on *buy*)

   What did you buy yesterday? (focus on *yesterday*)

C Complete the steps to practice question intonation.

1. In the chart below, write three questions about money or spending habits. Include real and unreal conditionals. Mark the intonation pattern in each question.
2. Interview other students in your class and note their answers.
3. Share what you learned from the interviews with a partner. In general, would you expect to see differences in how males and females answered your questions?

Questions	Interviewee 1	Interviewee 2	Interviewee 3

CRITICAL THINKING   Recognizing Pros and Cons

When you are making a decision or debating what to do, it can be helpful to discuss the pros and cons of a situation or action. Talking about the pros and cons can help you:

- make a better and more informed decision about the best action to take
- argue for (or against) a particular action more easily and effectively

EVERYDAY LANGUAGE   Discussing Pros and Cons

One advantage/disadvantage of … is that …
The upside/downside of … is that …
On the one/other hand, … is an obvious strength/weakness.

D   Work with a partner. Discuss the pros and cons of each of these situations.

1. paying for items with a credit card
2. going shopping with friends
3. eating out at restaurants
4. taking a vacation overseas

CRITICAL THINKING: RECOGNIZING PROS AND CONS

E   Work in a small group. Think about how stores can change shoppers' behavior. Complete the chart with some pros and cons of each action. Then compare your ideas with those of another group.

How to Change Shoppers' Behavior	Pros	Cons
Train sales clerks to smile more to put shoppers in a better mood.		
Bake fresh bread in a supermarket to make shoppers hungry.		
Post "limit 2 per customer" signs to suggest items are in limited supply.		
Move the registers so shoppers must walk through the whole store to pay.		
Put chairs outside the fitting rooms so people can sit while they wait.		

▲ **The interior of a department store, Berlin, Germany**

LESSON TASK Designing a Store Layout

A You have been asked to design the layout of a new store that will sell clothes for children, men, and women. Work in a small group to complete the steps.

1. Discuss what the store should include and where. Think about how the layout might affect the behavior of customers.
2. Draw your store plan on a separate piece of paper. Label each area on the floor plan.
   - women's clothing
   - men's clothing
   - children's clothing
   - fitting rooms
   - check-out area
   - entrance/exit
3. Share your design with the rest of the class. Explain what you will include and where and why. Then listen to the ideas of other groups.

B As a class, discuss the following questions.

CRITICAL THINKING: SYNTHESIZING

1. Of the store layouts in exercise A, which one is the most attractive? Why?
2. Which of the layouts would be least likely to appeal to people your age? Why?
3. Which of the layouts is the most unusual? Do you think the layout would work well in an actual store? Why or why not?

The Decoy Effect

A teenager makes popcorn at a refreshment stand in a movie theater in Denver, Colorado, USA.

BEFORE VIEWING

A Complete these definitions of words and phrases from the video with the best option from the box. When you have finished, check your answers with a partner.

appealing	decoy	influence	out of line
concession stand	head over	irresistible	rip off

1. If something is _____, it is so attractive that it is impossible not to like it.

2. A(n) _____ is a place that typically sells food inside a larger business.

3. A(n) _____ is something that people feel costs more than it should.

4. If a person decides to _____ somewhere, he or she goes or visits there.

5. If a person can _____ something, he or she can have an effect on it.

6. If something is _____, it goes beyond what most people would accept.

7. A(n) _____ is a thing or person designed to trick a person or animal.

8. If something is _____, people think it is nice, interesting, or desirable.

B Work in a small group. You are about to watch a video about refreshments that are sold at movie theaters. What refreshments are usually sold in your country? Do you buy refreshments at a movie theater? Why or why not?

WHILE VIEWING

C ▶ 1.1 Watch the video. Then, in a small group, choose the answer that best defines "the decoy effect."

UNDERSTANDING MAIN IDEAS

a. Customers are more likely to choose good value items if no decoy options are available.

b. Offering customers one more option can have a strong effect on which option they prefer.

c. If customers have several similarly priced options, they usually prefer the cheapest one.

D ▶ 1.1 Watch again. Complete the notes with one word or a number from the video.

UNDERSTANDING DETAILS

1st Experiment	• Customers had choice between sm. and lg. popcorn
	• Experiment showed that $_____ size was most popular 1
	• Some customers felt other size was a lot of _____ 2
2nd Experiment	• Consumers had choice of sm., _____ , or lg. popcorn 3
	• Experiment showed that $_____ one was most popular 4
	• Consumers explained that this size was a good _____ 5

AFTER VIEWING

E Work with a partner. Practice orally summarizing the video. Try to do it without looking at the notes in exercise D.

> *This video showed two experiments to illustrate the decoy effect in a movie theater. In the first experiment, . . .*

F Work with a partner. Discuss the questions. Then share your ideas with the class.

CRITICAL THINKING: REFLECTING

1. A decoy is a thing designed to trick a person or animal. Does this change how you feel about companies using the decoy effect? Why or why not?

2. Will you change your shopping behavior after learning about the decoy effect? If yes, what will you do differently? If no, why not?

3. What else do businesses do to encourage consumers to spend more?

B Vocabulary

MEANING FROM
CONTEXT **A** 🎧 **Track 8** Read and listen to the conversations. Notice the words in blue. Then complete
each definition with one of the answers in the box.

> an important task
> as much as is necessary
> a necessary but boring task
> causing somebody to be upset
> not currently available to buy
>
> information discovered through research
> support and commitment
> identifying as either male or female
> to do something such as an experiment
> to do things with other people

A: You didn't mark your **gender** on this application form, Bob.

B: I must have forgotten. Filling out applications is such a **chore**. Would you mind
checking the box next to "male" for me, please?

1. The noun *gender* means _____.

2. The noun *chore* means _____.

A: Is it true that you met Lionel Messi yesterday? For real?

B: Yeah! And it was great, especially because I speak some Spanish, so I could **interact**
with him better than the other people with me.

3. The verb *interact* means _____.

A: How did your experiment go, Ahmed?

B: I can't say for sure yet, but I came up with a good way to **conduct** it, I think, so I hope
the **findings** will be useful.

4. The verb *conduct* means _____.

5. The noun *findings* means _____.

A: Did you hear that Professor Albright has lost her job?

B: Yeah, and I'm upset about it. She's worked here for over 25 years apparently. I think
the college should have shown more **loyalty** to her.

6. The noun *loyalty* means _____.

A: How was your weekend, David?

B: Not so good. I went to the mall on a **mission** to buy a gift for my sister. I was there for
hours, but I couldn't find the right gift. It was pretty **frustrating**.

7. The noun *mission* means _____.

8. The adjective *frustrating* means _____.

A: Excuse me. Where could I find *Marketing Basics*?

B: Sorry to tell you this, but that book's **out of stock** just now. We thought we had
ordered **sufficient** copies, but more students purchased it than we expected.

9. The phrase *out of stock* means _____.

10. The adjective *sufficient* means _____.

Businesses often give loyalty cards to reward customers who make frequent purchases.

B Work with a partner. Discuss these questions. Provide reasons and examples to support your opinions.

PERSONALIZING

1. Are you familiar with loyalty cards? In your view, do loyalty cards really make people more loyal to a particular store or restaurant?
2. In your experience, what do you find to be the most frustrating thing about shopping?
3. What are some tasks that children generally consider to be chores, but which people often enjoy as they get older?

VOCABULARY SKILL Participial Adjectives

Participial adjectives are formed from the past (usually –*ed*) or present (–*ing*) participle of a verb. These two forms have different meanings and can be confused.

Typically, past participial adjectives describe an emotion or feeling that somebody has:

> He felt **frustrated** that the item was out of stock.
> Many people were **bored** during the discussion.

Present participial adjectives describe something that causes an emotion or feeling:

> He said that the item being out of stock was **frustrating**.
> The discussion was **boring** to many people.

C Choose the correct word to complete each question. Then interview people in your class and discuss your answers.

1. Which makes you more (frustrated / frustrating): when an item you want is out of stock or when it is too expensive to buy? Why?
2. Which sounds more (excited / exciting): interacting with older people from another country or with people your age from your country? Why?
3. Which would you find more (bored / boring): a documentary about loyalty or one about gender? Why?
4. Which option would make you more (relaxed / relaxing) after working all day: taking a bath or going for a walk? Why?
5. Which would you be more (interested / interesting) in doing: watching a movie or going to a party? Why?

Listening A Lecture about Consumer Behavior

Man and Woman Shopper at a Mall

Woman   Man

Mall Entrance

BEFORE LISTENING

A Discuss the questions with a partner. Then share your ideas and reasons with the class.

1. Look at the image. Do you think it is intended to be serious or humorous? Why? Do you think it makes a real point about the difference in how men and women shop?
2. What frustrates you when shopping?
3. The professor discusses a research study titled "Men Buy, Women Shop." What do you think this title most likely means?

WHILE LISTENING

B 🎧 **Track 9** Listen to the lecture. Take notes as you listen. Then answer the questions. When you have finished, compare answers with a partner.

1. What subject do you think this professor is teaching?

   a. Marketing: the study of how businesses interact with customers
   b. Psychology: the study of how and why people think and behave
   c. Sociology: the study of how people generally behave in society

2. What do the speakers suggest "Men Buy, Women Shop" most likely means?

   a. Both men and women like shopping, but only men enjoy purchasing items.
   b. For women, shopping is more than just buying an item; for men, the focus is on buying an item.
   c. Men enjoy spending money, but women prefer searching for items to buy.

3. What is the main purpose of the study?
   a. To compare online shopping with in-store experiences
   b. To describe what all men and women do when shopping
   c. To provide data on trends for marketing purposes

C 🎧 **Track 10** Listen to part of the lecture. Take notes as you listen, dividing them for men and women. Then answer the question below. When you have finished, compare answers with a partner.

According to the study, which statements apply to men shoppers, and which ones apply to women shoppers? Put a check (✔) in the correct column.

	Men	Women
1. Become frustrated if store employees are inefficient		
2. Dislike having to wait in a long line to pay for an item		
3. Get upset when sales assistants are not easy to find		
4. May be concerned about the availability of parking		
5. Want store clerks to be polite and knowledgeable		

AFTER LISTENING

D Work with a partner. Discuss these questions.

1. Do you think the frustrations mentioned in exercise C are unique to men and to women? Why or why not?
2. How might the information in the lecture be useful for businesses in terms of store design and sales associate training?

E Work in a small group to complete the steps. Then share your ideas with the class.

1. Make a list of questions you would ask consumers today to find out about their shopping habits.
2. Have each member of your group answer the questions.
3. Discuss how your group's responses would help you plan a marketing campaign.

▼ **A customer looks at smartphones in Stockholm, Sweden.**

B Speaking

SPEAKING SKILL Quoting Statistics

Statistics or other numerical data can make your arguments easier to understand and believe. There are three common ways to quote statistics:

1. As a percentage or proportion of something

*According to the survey, only **30 percent of shoppers** were female.*
*The findings show that just **three in ten consumers** were satisfied.*

2. As a multiple of some other number

*After 2015, sales increased **three times** as much as the year before.*
*The number of customers **tripled** after the company lowered prices.*

3. As a number

*The company announced that it would open **three** new locations.*
*There are over **220 million** online shoppers in the United States.*

A ⌂ **Track 11** Work in a small group. Guess which statistic from the box best completes the infographic and fill in the circles. Then listen to a conversation and check your answers.

20	46%	60%	68%	80%

Statistics about Consumer Behavior

◯ 1. Percentage of consumers who have not completed a purchase because of poor service

2. Shoppers are this many times more likely to share a bad experience than keep quiet about it ◯

◯ 3. Percentage of people worldwide who say they prefer to spend as little time grocery shopping as possible

4. Percentage of people in North America who enjoy finding a bargain ◯

◯ 5. Approximate percentage of Americans who research a product online before buying it

PERSONALIZING **B** Work with a partner. Which situations in exercise A have you experienced?

C Work with a partner. Interview each other and make a note of your answers.

1. Do you prefer shopping alone? ☐ Yes ☐ No
2. Do you shop in stores more often than online? ☐ Yes ☐ No
3. Have you written an online review? ☐ Yes ☐ No
4. Do you do research online before buying an expensive item? ☐ Yes ☐ No

D As a class, tally the answers for each of the questions in exercise C. Then use that information to answer the questions below. Are you surprised by any of the results?

QUOTING STATISTICS

1. _____ percent of the people in our class prefer shopping alone.

2. _____ percent of us shop in stores instead of online.

3. _____ students have written at least one online review.

4. In our class, _____ percent do online research before making an expensive purchase.

FINAL TASK Giving a Persuasive Presentation

> You are going to deliver an "elevator pitch." This is a short talk designed to persuade somebody to buy or invest in something. The name comes from the idea that if you were to meet a potential investor in an elevator, you should be able to deliver your whole talk before the elevator completes its journey. This is typically 60 seconds or less.

A Work with a partner. Brainstorm a smartphone app (a software application) that would help shoppers in some way, such as by solving a problem that many shoppers have. Discuss your app's benefits, features, price, and name.

BRAINSTORMING

As part of a class assignment, a marketing student practices giving a pitch to a bank executive in an elevator.

A rhetorical question is one that does not require an answer. When giving a presentation, rhetorical questions can be useful in several ways:

1. They can help you create a connection with the audience.
   We've all wanted an app like this, haven't we?

2. They can persuade the audience to agree with your view.
   Don't you think this new app sounds amazing?

3. They can introduce a point that you will then discuss.
   Why is the app going to be popular? Let me tell you.

B Complete the steps.

1. Create a plan for a 60-second elevator pitch to persuade others that your app would be useful. Think about statistics you could mention and rhetorical questions you could ask.
2. Practice giving your elevator pitch until you are confident that you can deliver your talk in 60 seconds or less.

PRESENTING **C** In a small group, deliver your pitch and answer any questions. Then listen to the other pitches. Which of the apps do you think would be the most useful to shoppers and why?

REFLECTION

1. What skill from this unit will help you present more effectively in the future?

   _____

   _____

2. What is the most interesting thing about how shoppers behave that you learned in this unit?

   _____

   _____

3. Here are the vocabulary words from the unit. Check (✓) the ones you can use.

☐ addictive	☐ complex AWL	☐ loyalty
☐ alter AWL	☐ conduct AWL	☐ mission
☐ assume AWL	☐ consumer AWL	☐ out of stock
☐ bargain	☐ findings	☐ purchase AWL
☐ bump	☐ frustrating	☐ retail
☐ chore	☐ gender AWL	☐ sufficient AWL
☐ commercial	☐ interact AWL	

MOTHER NATURE

2

A two-toed sloth mother hangs from a tree with her baby at the Aviarios Sloth Sanctuary, Costa Rica.

ACADEMIC SKILLS

LISTENING   Listening for Content Words
             Noting Who Says What
SPEAKING   Making Suggestions
             Syllable Stress before Suffixes
CRITICAL THINKING Deciding on Criteria

THINK AND DISCUSS

1 Look at the photo. How would you describe a sloth?

2 As the title "Mother Nature" shows, nature is seen as female in English. Does the word for nature have a gender in your language? What is it?

Look at the photos and read the information. Then discuss the questions.

1. How do bees help flowers reproduce?

2. The baby kangaroo is protected in its mother's pouch for about 10 months. In what other ways do animals protect their young?

3. The life cycle of a salmon is several years. What other animals have short life cycles? What animals have long life cycles?

4. What information was the most surprising to you?

CYCLE OF LIFE

▶ Newborn kangaroos, or joeys, are one inch (2.5 centimeters) long at birth and spend their first four months living in the protection of the mother's pouch. Then the joey begins to leave the pouch for short trips to eat grass. At 10 months, the joey is mature enough to leave the mother's pouch for good.

▲ This bee covered with the flower's pollen plays a key role in transferring pollen from one plant to another. Many plants reproduce through this process of pollination, with flowers attracting bees with colors and smells.

▶ Bears are just one of the challenges that these adult salmon face. They are swimming upstream in Alaska to return to their place of birth. Some fish never make it due to predators or exhaustion. Adults that reach their destination will reproduce by laying and fertilizing eggs, and then will die. The baby fish will swim out to sea, where they will live for two or three years. Then they will return to their freshwater birthplace, starting the life cycle all over again.

Vocabulary

A 🎧 **Track 12** Look at the photo and read the caption. Then read and listen to the information. Notice each word in blue and think about its meaning.

King penguins in tall snowy grass in the spring in the Antarctic

THE KING PENGUIN: Challenges to Reproduction

Many islands in the Antarctic such as the Possession Islands have huge **colonies** of king penguins. These birds come to the islands to **reproduce**. Although scientists believe the worldwide population is increasing and king penguins are not in danger of **extinction**, individual birds often have to **struggle** to stay alive.

Weather is one **challenge** that the birds face. This far south, cold temperatures make it hard to keep eggs warm. Female birds share this **responsibility** with their mate. Perhaps surprisingly, climate change can also **threaten** the birds. After eggs hatch, parents feed their chicks. Warmer oceans mean less food nearby. As a result, chicks are left unprotected for longer periods while their parents hunt.

Another **factor** is space. Some colonies have 100,000 or more birds, each of which must find and defend a **territory** of less than three feet (one meter) across. **Predators** are another challenge. Adults must protect young penguins from seals and other sea mammals, and sometimes even from other birds.

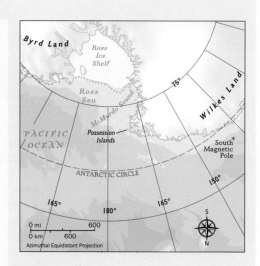

B Write each word in blue from exercise A next to its definition.

1. _____ (n) a duty that a person or animal has

2. _____ (n) when a species of animal or plant is no longer alive

3. _____ (n) an area of land that belongs to a certain animal

4. _____ (n) animals that eat other animals

5. _____ (n) groups of animals living together in one area

6. _____ (n) something difficult that requires great effort

7. _____ (n) something that partly causes or contributes to a situation

8. _____ (v) to cause danger to

9. _____ (v) to fight or work hard to achieve something

10. _____ (v) to have babies

C Read the statements. Write T for *True* or F for *False*. Then use a dictionary to confirm your answers and correct the false statements.

1. _____ *Extinct* is the adjective form of *extinction*.

2. _____ *Challenge* and *struggle* can be either nouns or verbs.

3. _____ *Colony*, *territory*, and *factor* do not have plural forms.

4. _____ *Threaten* does not have a noun form.

5. _____ *Responsible* is the adjective form of *responsibility*.

D Complete these sentences with the correct form of one of the words in the box. More than one answer may be possible.

challenge	factor	responsibility	struggle	threaten

1. Most people _____ to manage their time.

2. People must always be fully _____ for their actions.

3. Having close friends is a _____ in whether people are happy.

4. People face fewer _____ in life now than in the past.

5. Technology _____ people's relationships with others.

E Work with a partner. Discuss the questions.

1. Do you agree or disagree with each statement in exercise D? Explain.
2. Is there a statement that you and your partner disagree on? Change the sentence so that you both agree with it.

CRITICAL THINKING: EVALUATING

A Listening A Panel about a Film Contest

National Geographic filmmaker Bertie Gregory films a baby goat at a farm in Uttarakhand, India.

BEFORE LISTENING

CRITICAL THINKING:
EVALUATING

A Before you listen to the discussion, answer these questions with a partner.

1. In what ways do documentaries differ from other films?
2. Nature is one common subject for documentaries. What other subjects are common?
3. In general, documentaries are less popular than typical Hollywood movies. Why do you think this is?

WHILE LISTENING

LISTENING FOR
MAIN IDEAS

B 🎧 **Track 13** ▶ **2.1** Listen to the discussion. Then choose the statement that best summarizes what you heard.

a. Some film students are comparing two nature documentaries.
b. Some filmmakers are talking about the best subject for a nature documentary.
c. Some people are discussing a winning nature documentary.

If you listen to a conversation or a talk with more than one speaker, it is helpful to note which speaker says what. This is especially true if the speakers express different opinions about a topic. Use abbreviations in your notes to indicate which speaker's opinion you are noting. For example, you could use *M* for Man, *W1* for first woman, or the initials of a person's name, such as *BG* for Bertie Gregory.

C 🎧 **Track 13** Listen again. Take notes about each speaker's opinions. Use abbreviations to note who says what. Then use your notes to decide who expressed the opinions below. Write the speaker's initial: *A* for Abdul, *M* for Martha, or *S* for Shannon.

NOTE TAKING

a. _____ There was some effective camerawork and filmmaking.

b. _____ The director did a good job showing the island's climate.

c. _____ The film had moments of danger, humor, and seriousness.

d. _____ The scenes of predators' attacks were hard to watch but necessary to include.

e. _____ The film's music did not match the images on screen.

f. _____ The scenes showing the size of the colony were impressive.

AFTER LISTENING

D Form a small group. Discuss these questions.

PERSONALIZING

1. Would you be interested in watching *The Penguins of Possession Island*? Explain.
2. What documentaries have you watched that you would recommend? Why would you recommend them?
3. In general, do you prefer watching documentaries or other types of movies? Why?

CRITICAL THINKING Deciding on Criteria

When evaluating or deciding something, it is helpful to consider the most important aspects. These are called *criteria* (singular: *criterion*). For example, to choose the winning documentary, the speakers' three criteria were the quality of the camerawork, filmmaking, and music.

E Work with a partner. Follow the steps below. Take notes in your notebook.

CRITICAL THINKING: DECIDING ON CRITERIA

1. Think of a situation you might need to make a decision about. It could be a major or minor decision such as choosing which movie to see with friends, where to attend college, or whom to marry.
2. Brainstorm some criteria you would use to make a decision about it.
3. Decide on the top five criteria, and rank them from most to least important.

F With your partner, present your criteria to the class, but do not mention what situation you are making a decision about. Your classmates will try to infer the situation from your criteria.

A Speaking

PRONUNCIATION Syllable Stress before Suffixes

🎧 **Track 14** When suffixes –*ic*, –*ity*, and –*tion* are added to words, the syllable stress changes. The primary stress is on the syllable before the suffix.

romance + –ic → ro**man**tic

possible + –ity → possi**bil**ity

educate + –tion → edu**ca**tion

A 🎧 **Track 15** For each word, mark the syllable that you think will have the strongest stress. Then listen to check your answers.

1. academic
2. reproduction
3. responsibility
4. complexity
5. frustration
6. interaction

B Work with a partner. Mark the stressed syllable in each word. Then practice saying each word with the correct syllable stress pattern.

Suffix: –*ic*	Suffix: –*ity*	Suffix: –*tion*
automatic	capacity	construction
domestic	community	information
dynamic	flexibility	motivation
specific	priority	reaction
genetic	electricity	extinction

CRITICAL THINKING:
INTERPRETING A
FLOWCHART

C 🎧 **Track 16** Work in a small group. Study the flowchart on the next page about cloning, which is a technology-assisted form of reproduction. Discuss where the following statements should be added to the chart. Write the statements in the chart. Then check your answers by listening to an instructor explain cloning.

The resulting baby is a clone of the first animal.
A body cell is removed from an adult animal.
Scientists remove the nucleus from that cell.
Chemicals or electricity make the egg divide.

CLONING AN ANIMAL FROM AN ADULT CELL

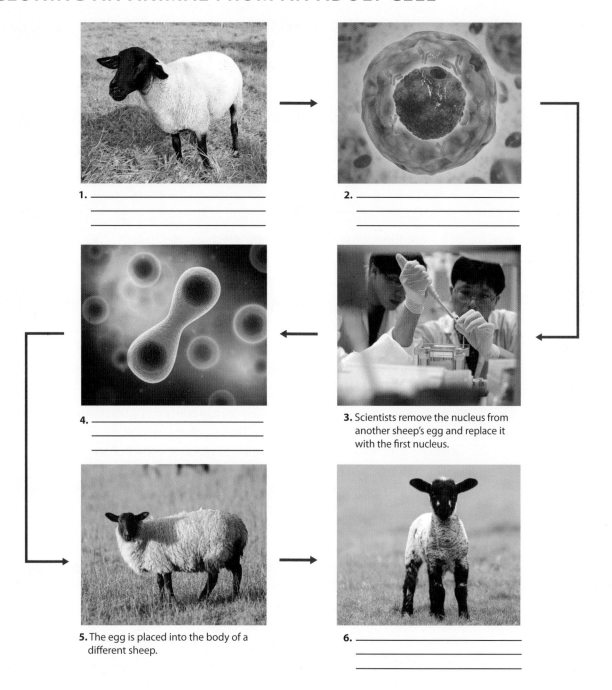

1. _____

2. _____

3. Scientists remove the nucleus from another sheep's egg and replace it with the first nucleus.

4. _____

5. The egg is placed into the body of a different sheep.

6. _____

D Form a small group and discuss the questions.

CRITICAL THINKING: EVALUATING

1. Which of these, if any, do you feel are good reasons for cloning animals? Why?
   - to bring back particular dead animals such as much-loved pets
   - to bring back extinct species such as *Tyrannosaurus Rex* or other dinosaurs
   - to copy animals with certain characteristics such as fast racehorses
   - to produce animals with characteristics that benefit humans
   - to save endangered species such as some types of sea turtles

2. If it were possible for scientists to bring back just one extinct species through cloning, what criteria would you use to decide which species to bring back?

GRAMMAR FOR SPEAKING Adjective Clauses

An adjective clause (also called a relative clause) describes or modifies a noun. We can join two simple sentences together by using an adjective clause.

> I saw a documentary. <u>It</u> was about king penguins. →
> I saw a documentary **which/that** <u>was about king penguins.</u>

If the relative pronoun is the subject of the clause, use *who* or *that* for people. Use *that* or *which* for animals or things.

> The film showed predators. <u>They</u> attacked young penguins. →
> The film showed predators **that/which** <u>attacked young penguins.</u>

Sometimes, the relative pronoun is the object of the clause. Object relative pronouns are *whom* (or *who* in informal language), *that*, and *which*.

> I watched the documentary. You mentioned <u>it</u> to me. →
> I watched the documentary **that/which** <u>you mentioned to me.</u>

Note: When the relative pronoun is an object, it is often omitted, especially in informal use.

> I watched the documentary you mentioned to me.

E With a partner, take turns forming adjective clauses from these sentences. More than one answer may be possible.

1. King penguins live in large colonies. These may contain 100,000 birds.
2. These penguins have many predators. These include birds and seals.
3. Cloning is a technique. It allows scientists to produce copies of animals.
4. To clone, scientists use a cell. The cell has been taken from an adult animal.
5. Ken Burns is a filmmaker. He is best known for his history documentaries.
6. Many of his films are about important events. These events changed history.
7. I went to the documentary film festival. You told me about it.

CRITICAL THINKING: EVALUATING

F Discuss the following question in a small group. What criteria must a film or person meet in order to win an award in one of these categories?

- Criteria for best documentary: _____

_____

- Criteria for best director: _____

_____

A: *I think best documentary should be a film that tells an interesting true story.*
B: *Right, but it also needs to be a film that has amazing camerawork, don't you think?*
C: *Sure. But for me, the most important criterion is that it should challenge my thinking.*

LESSON TASK Discussing Conservation and Extinction

◄ **The number of giant pandas in the wild has been rising in China. The population has grown due to increased protection from hunters and expansion of protected habitat.**

EVERYDAY LANGUAGE Asking for Repetition

More Formal: *Could you say that again?*   Less Formal: *Come again?*
I missed that, I'm afraid.   *What's that?*
Sorry. I didn't catch that.   *Sorry?*

A Work in a small group. Discuss what factors can lead to the extinction of a species. Use different ways to ask for repetition if necessary.

A: *I think that some species go extinct because of climate change.*
B: *Sorry. I didn't catch that.*
A: *I said climate change can cause some species to go extinct.*

B In your group, rank these ideas in order from most important (1) to least important (4) as reasons in favor of species conservation.

CRITICAL THINKING: RANKING

_____ Some endangered species provide economic benefits (e.g., ecotourism).
_____ The extinction of one plant or animal can affect other plants and animals.
_____ Some endangered species could be a source of medicine for humans.
_____ Humans share Earth with other species; every species deserves to live.

C In your group, complete these steps. Make notes about your ideas.

PRESENTING

1. Decide on a plant or animal species to discuss.
2. Discuss how life would be affected if this species suddenly went extinct.
3. Discuss what humans could do to make sure this species does not become extinct.

D Select one group member to present your ideas to the class. Say which species you chose and why it is important, what might happen if it went extinct, and how humans could conserve it.

Video

A rare Kemp's ridley sea turtle swims near Cocos Island off the coast of Costa Rica.

Costa Rica

Turtles under Threat

BEFORE VIEWING

A In Lesson A, you explored challenges to a species' survival. In this video, you will learn about a low-tech way to save one species of sea turtle. Before you watch, discuss the questions below with a partner.

1. The Kemp's ridley sea turtle is the most endangered of all sea turtles. What human activities do you think threaten it?
2. In addition to the threats posed by humans, what other challenges do these turtles probably face?

B Complete these sentences to define words from the video. Then mark the adjective clause in each sentence.

biologists	exclude	population	species
device	marine		

1. A group of animals that can reproduce with one another is called a(n) _____.
2. The _____ of a species is all the individuals that are members of that species.
3. _____ creatures such as sharks and shrimp are animals that live in the sea.
4. Scientists who study life and living organisms are called _____.
5. People usually _____ something that they neither want nor need.
6. A machine or tool that has a special function is called a(n) _____.

WHILE VIEWING

C ▶ 2.2 Watch the video. Then answer each question.

UNDERSTANDING
MAIN IDEAS

1. What is the Turtle Excluder Device?
   a. a new type of fishing net
   b. an improved fishing boat

2. Why is the device needed?
   a. to help marine species reproduce
   b. to protect one kind of sea turtle

3. How does the device work?
   a. It separates large animals from small ones.
   b. It lets fishermen see what they have caught.

4. In the United States, who must use the device?
   a. biologists who study sharks and turtles
   b. fishermen who mostly catch shrimp

D ▶ 2.2 Watch the video again and take notes in the T-chart about the advantages and disadvantages of the Turtle Excluder Device.

NOTE TAKING

Disadvantage(s) to Fishermen (according to some fishermen)	Advantage(s) to Fishermen (according to biologists)

AFTER VIEWING

E Work in a small group. Complete these steps.

CRITICAL THINKING:
SYNTHESIZING

1. Predict some questions and concerns that fishermen might have about using the Turtle Excluder Device.
2. Come up with answers to these questions and concerns that would make fishermen feel positive about using the device.
3. Join with another group. Share the questions and concerns you predicted and the answers you came up with.

Vocabulary

A 🎧 **Track 17** Look at the photo and read the caption. Then read and listen to the interview. Notice each word in **blue** and think about its meaning.

ALL ABOUT ORCHIDS

Host: Joining me today is Dr. Sam Darrow, a botanist[1] who **specializes** in the study of orchids. Welcome, Dr. Darrow. So, tell me: what factors led to your interest in orchids?

Dr. Darrow: When I was a child, my father grew orchids at home. At first, I loved them for their beauty. But over time, I noticed how amazing they are.

Host: Amazing? How?

Dr. Darrow: Well, like every living **organism**, orchids need to reproduce. Their **primary** way to do this is to **manufacture** nectar, which insects love. When insects visit orchids and **consume** this sweet liquid, they get covered in pollen. This is a **substance** that contains DNA. The insects **transfer** this DNA to other orchids, and reproduction can take place.

Host: So, that's an interesting **method**: use something sweet to attract insects in order to reproduce. What other ways do they attract insects?

Dr. Darrow: One species of orchids smells like dirty diapers[2]. To us, this scent is unpleasant, but it's attractive to some insects. And *Epidendrum* orchids **resemble** milkweed, a favorite food of butterflies, but actually aren't food at all.

Host: So it's a trick.

Dr. Darrow: Right! Butterflies visit expecting food, but get only pollen. Other orchids play different tricks. Some look like typical places where insects make homes or find **shelter** during bad weather. Insects visit, get covered with pollen, but soon leave when they find out the flowers are not good places to live.

Host: Thank you, Dr. Darrow. I've learned a lot.

An *Epidendrum* orchid is pollinated by a butterfly.

[1] **botanist** (n): a scientist who specializes in the study of plants
[2] **diaper** (n): a type of underwear for babies

Context clues can help you understand the meaning of words and phrases as well as their part of speech. Context clues can be found in the words and phrases around a particular word.

> One species of orchids smells like dirty diapers. To us, this **scent** is unpleasant, but it's attractive to some insects.

The context clues *smells, dirty diapers, unpleasant,* and *attractive* help us understand that *scent* probably means a smell. The word *this* before *scent* tells us that *scent* is a noun.

B With a partner, use context clues to decide whether each word in blue in exercise A is a noun, verb, or adjective.

C Read the descriptions. Use context clues to write a definition of each bold word. Then check your definitions in a dictionary.

In nature, some predators **specialize** in hunting a particular species. To protect themselves from these attacks, some species **resemble** something else. For example, stick insects look like small sticks. This **method** of protection works because predators think they are part of a tree, not something to eat.

1. To specialize means to _____.

2. To resemble means to _____.

3. A method is a(n) _____.

Some species of penguins **consume** a lot of krill, which are tiny sea **organisms** that look like shrimp. Krill are among the most abundant species in the world. The **primary** foods consumed by king penguins, however, are fish and squid.

4. To consume means to _____.

5. An organism is a(n) _____.

6. Primary means _____.

Crabs use a **substance** called calcium carbonate to **manufacture** a hard shell. This shell covers and protects their body. Hermit crabs, in contrast, cannot produce their own shell and must use one produced by another organism for **shelter**. As a hermit crab grows and its borrowed shell becomes too small, it simply **transfers** itself to a larger one.

7. A substance is a(n) _____.

8. To manufacture means to _____.

9. Shelter is _____.

10. To transfer means to _____.

Listening A Conversation on Campus

This red air plant is an epiphyte.

BEFORE LISTENING

> **LISTENING SKILL** Listening for Content Words
>
> 🎧 **Track 18** Content words, which are usually nouns and verbs, carry most of the meaning in a sentence. Speakers usually emphasize content words slightly more than other words.
>
> > *When I was a **child**, my **father** grew **orchids** at **home**. At first, I **loved** them for their **beauty**. But over **time**, I **noticed** how **amazing** they are.*
>
> Because content words are stressed more, you can concentrate on listening for them. This is helpful because if you understand the content words, you will generally have a good idea of what a speaker is talking about.

A 🎧 **Track 19** Read the beginning of a conversation between two people. Mark the words that you think are the content words. Then listen to see which words are stressed.

Leo: Excuse me? Sorry to bother you, but do you know the way to the conservatory greenhouse? This map isn't helping me much.

Elena: Yeah, the map isn't great and the campus does resemble a maze, doesn't it? Anyway, you're in luck. I'm actually on my way to the conservatory greenhouse right now. We can walk together.

WHILE LISTENING

B 🎧 **Track 20** Listen to the whole conversation. Then answer the questions.

LISTENING FOR
MAIN IDEAS

1. Who are the two speakers?
   a. professors
   b. scientists
   c. students

2. What do they mainly discuss?
   a. how to get somewhere
   b. what a lecture may cover
   c. what somebody is like

3. What kind of organisms do they mostly discuss?
   a. insects
   b. epiphytes
   c. trees

C 🎧 **Track 21** Listen again to part of the conversation. Then answer the questions. Mark T for *True*, F for *False*, or NG if the information is *Not Given*.

LISTENING FOR
DETAILS

	T	F	NG
1. Leo, the male student, is new to the campus.	T	F	NG
2. Elena, the female student, knows a lot about epiphytes.	T	F	NG
3. Elena is in her second year of college.	T	F	NG
4. Epiphytes are plants that get water from the air.	T	F	NG
5. Epiphytes usually grow in places with a humid climate.	T	F	NG
6. Many varieties of epiphytes grow in Florida.	T	F	NG
7. Professor Darrow rarely studies orchids or epiphytes.	T	F	NG

AFTER LISTENING

D Work in a small group. Discuss the questions.

CRITICAL THINKING:
REFLECTING

1. When you are lost, are you comfortable asking a stranger for directions? Why or why not?

2. In general, are you comfortable talking to people you don't know? Why or why not?

3. What are some situations in which you might need to begin a conversation with a stranger? What strategies could you use to start talking to that person?

4. Would you be interested in taking a class that focuses on plant life? Why or why not?

5. Why is it important to study how plants survive in a variety of conditions? What useful information can we learn?

B Speaking

College students in
Jeddah, Saudi Arabia

BRAINSTORMING **A** Work with a partner. Look at the idea map and add one more common challenge. Then brainstorm at least two possible solutions for each one and add them to the map.

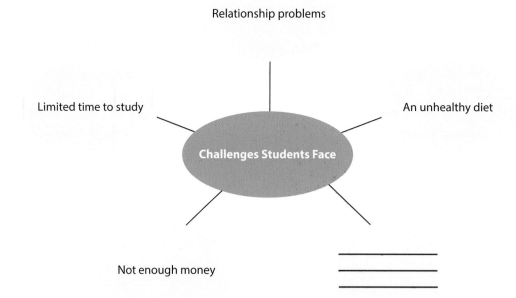

Relationship problems

Limited time to study

An unhealthy diet

Challenges Students Face

Not enough money

There are several expressions you can use to make a suggestion to someone.

Why don't you go …?

Have you considered doing …?

You could take …

You should make …

I recommend talking …

I suggest that you get …

To make a suggestion less strong, use an adverb like *maybe* or *perhaps*. To make a suggestion stronger, use an adverb like *strongly* or *really*.

Maybe you could leave …

Perhaps you should go …

I **really** recommend doing …

I **strongly** suggest that you plan …

B Interview several students in your class. Take turns asking which of the problems from exercise A they have experienced and make suggestions.

C Work with a partner you did not interview in exercise B. Take turns sharing some of the best suggestions you were given.

FINAL TASK Creating and Presenting a Proposal

> You are going to create and present a short proposal for a 10-minute nature documentary.

A Work with two or three students. Brainstorm answers to the following questions. When making your decisions, you may find it helpful to discuss key criteria first.

BRAINSTORMING

- What species will our documentary be about? Why?
- What aspect of this species' life will we focus on? Why?
- What will be the main scenes in our documentary? Why?
- Which country or countries will we need to travel to? Why?
- What will be unique or special about our documentary?

B In your group, make a presentation plan by answering the following questions.

ORGANIZING INFORMATION

- In what order will we present information about our documentary? Why?
- Who will present which information? (Everyone in your group should speak.)
- How will we present the information? For example, will we use visuals, create slides, or write anything on the board? Why or why not?

PRESENTATION SKILL   Presenting with Others

Before your group presentation, select a member to be a time-keeper. This will help you keep to your time limit and not go off topic. Decide on a signal that the time-keeper can give.

When you introduce your group presentation, let your audience know who will say what and when:

> First, Ahmed will talk about . . .
>
> Then Maria will discuss . . .
>
> And finally, I'll cover . . .

It also helps your audience if you give clear transitions between each speaker:

> Now I'm going to hand this over to Maria, who'll give more information about . . .
>
> Next Alex is going to discuss some important points about . . .

C After you have made your plan, practice your presentation. Make sure you include an introduction of your group members and transitions between speakers.

PRESENTING   **D** As a group, present information about your proposed documentary to the class. After your presentation, invite the class to ask questions or make suggestions about how your documentary could be improved.

E As a class, talk about what you liked about the documentary proposals, and why. Then vote on which were the best three documentary ideas.

REFLECTION

1. What specific skill that you learned in this unit is the most useful one for you? Why?

_____

_____

2. Has your attitude toward wild animals changed in any way after studying this unit? Explain.

_____

_____

3. Here are the vocabulary words from the unit. Check (✓) the ones you can use.

☐ challenge AWL   ☐ organism   ☐ specialize

☐ colony   ☐ predator   ☐ struggle

☐ consume AWL   ☐ primary AWL   ☐ substance

☐ extinction   ☐ reproduce   ☐ territory

☐ factor AWL   ☐ resemble   ☐ threaten

☐ manufacture   ☐ responsibility ☐ transfer AWL

☐ method AWL   ☐ shelter

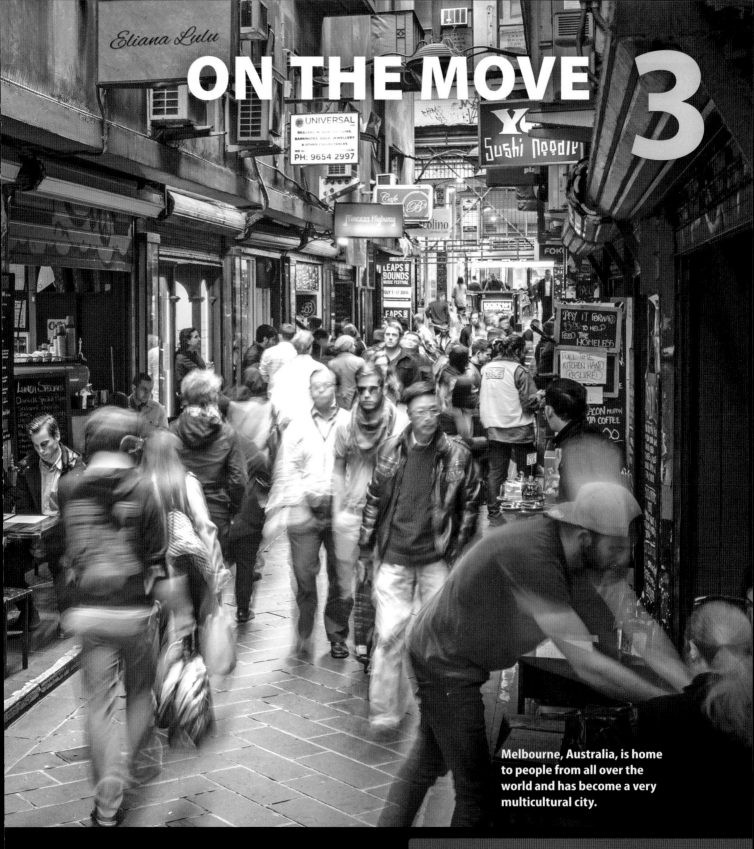

Eliana Lulu

ON THE MOVE 3

Melbourne, Australia, is home to people from all over the world and has become a very multicultural city.

ACADEMIC SKILLS

LISTENING	Listening for the Order of Events
	Noting Contrasting Ideas
SPEAKING	Expressing Probability
	Linking
CRITICAL THINKING	Categorizing Information

THINK AND DISCUSS

1. Why do you think people might have moved to Melbourne, Australia? What may have attracted them to the city?
2. Multicultural means representing many nationalities or ethnic groups. Describe a multicultural area in a city that you are familiar with.

HUMAN MIGRATION

EXPLORE THE THEME

Look at the map and key and read the captions. Then answer the questions.

1. What do the arrows and circles show?
2. Which two cities receive the greatest number of immigrants?
3. Which two cities have the largest proportion of residents who are immigrants?
4. Why do you think the cities on the map are called gateway cities?

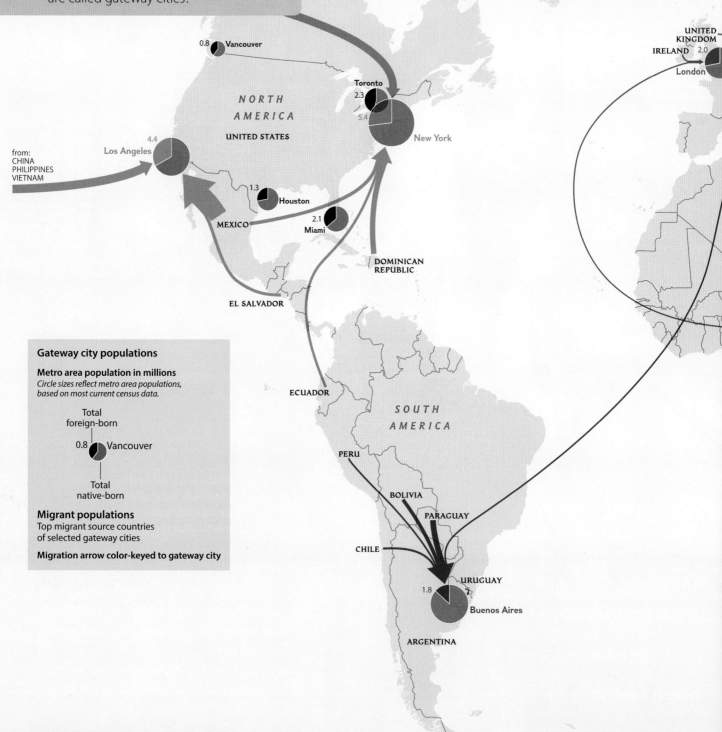

UNITED KINGDOM
IRELAND 2.0
London

0.8 Vancouver

NORTH AMERICA
UNITED STATES

Toronto
2.3
5.4
New York

from:
CHINA
PHILIPPINES
VIETNAM

4.4
Los Angeles

1.3
Houston

MEXICO

2.1
Miami

DOMINICAN REPUBLIC

EL SALVADOR

ECUADOR

SOUTH AMERICA

PERU

BOLIVIA

PARAGUAY

CHILE

URUGUAY

1.8
Buenos Aires

ARGENTINA

Gateway city populations

Metro area population in millions
Circle sizes reflect metro area populations, based on most current census data.

Total
foreign-born

0.8 ● Vancouver

Total
native-born

Migrant populations
Top migrant source countries of selected gateway cities

Migration arrow color-keyed to gateway city

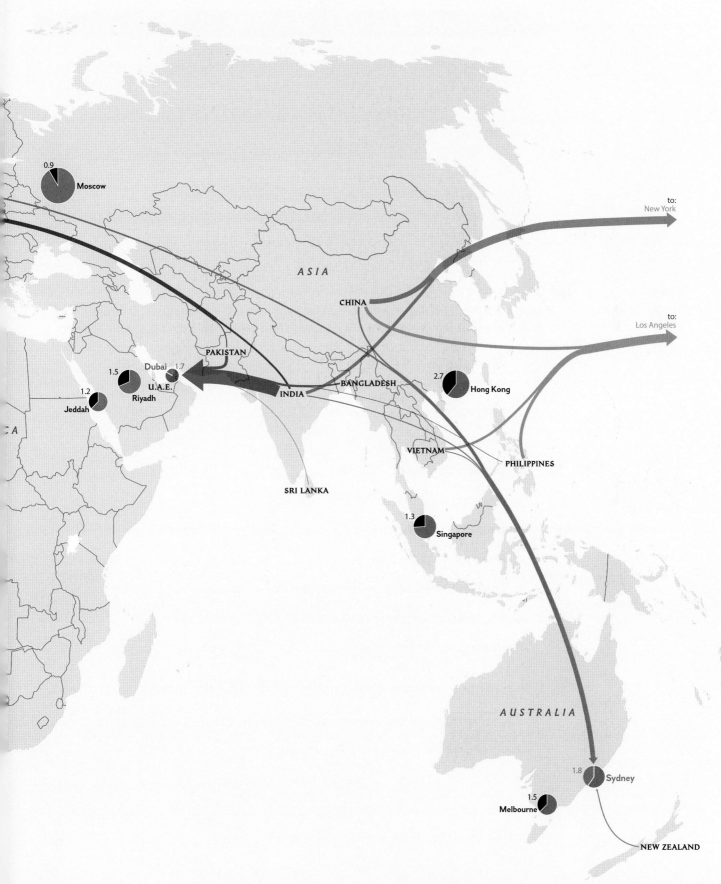

Moscow 0.9

Jeddah 1.2

Riyadh 1.5

Dubai 1.7
U.A.E.

PAKISTAN

ASIA

CHINA

INDIA

BANGLADESH

SRI LANKA

VIETNAM

PHILIPPINES

Hong Kong 2.7

Singapore 1.3

to:
New York

to:
Los Angeles

AUSTRALIA

Sydney 1.8

Melbourne 1.5

NEW ZEALAND

A Vocabulary

Writers and speakers sometimes use clues to help readers and listeners understand unfamiliar vocabulary. Learn to recognize the ways that writers and speakers do this.

1. By giving a synonym (or antonym) of a word
   Some airports mainly handle <u>domestic</u>, or <u>internal</u>, flights.

2. By defining a word
   Some airports mainly handle <u>domestic</u> flights. This means <u>ones within the country, but not international ones</u>.

3. By giving an explanation or example to clarify a word's meaning
   Some airports mainly handle <u>domestic</u> flights, which are generally <u>flights between a country's major cities</u>.

MEANING FROM CONTEXT

A 🎧 **Track 22** Listen to five short excerpts from a lecture you will hear later. Think about what each word in **blue** means. Listen for synonyms or explanations. Complete each definition with one word from the excerpt. Then listen again to check your answers.

1. a. **Settle** means to move to a new country or _____ and make a home there.

   b. **Voluntary** describes something that _____ have freely chosen to do.

2. a. **Emigration** means movement _____ from one place.

   b. **Immigration** means movement _____ somewhere.

3. a. **Nation** is another word for _____ .

   b. **Domestic** migration is _____ , within one country.

4. a. **Stability** is a political or _____ situation that is certain or safe.

   b. **Discrimination** occurs when people treat a _____ unfairly.

5. a. **Migrants** are people who have moved from one region to a new _____ .

   b. **Barrier** means some kind of _____ that people must overcome.

B With a partner, answer the questions. Then use a dictionary to confirm your answers.

1. What noun means a place where people settle? _____

2. What verb means to do something voluntarily? _____

3. What are the verb forms of *emigration* and *immigration*? _____

4. What is the adjective form of *stability*? _____

5. What verb means the thing that migrants do? _____

Workers from Romania at an apple orchard in Spain.

ROMANIA

C Read the article and fill in the blanks with the correct word from exercise A. Two of the words from exercise A will not be used.

MIGRATION IN ROMANIA

Romania is the largest _____ in southeastern Europe. It has a population
                        1

of around 20 million people. At the end of the last century, Romania saw a lot of

_____ migration. People moved from the countryside to large cities such
     2

as Bucharest. Since joining the European Union in 2007, migration out of the country

has become more common. Studies show that up to 2.5 million Romanians have

made a(n) _____ choice to leave the country in recent years. Some of these
            3

people have chosen to _____ in Spain and Italy. Because Romanian is a
                        4

Romance language like Spanish and Italian, the language _____ in these
                                                          5

countries may be easier for Romanian _____ to overcome. In addition
                                       6

to _____ from Romania, over a quarter of a million people have moved
     7

into the country recently. Most of this _____ comes from the Republic
                                          8

of Moldova, a small country that borders Romania and has Romanian as its official

language.

D Discuss these questions in a small group.

1. If you could settle in any nation in the world, where would you choose?
2. Are you more interested in domestic news or international news?
3. What is one barrier to learning English that you are working to overcome?

Listening A Lecture about Migration

BEFORE LISTENING

PREDICTING   **A**   Work in a small group. You will hear a lecture in which a professor discusses some reasons why people migrate. Look at the photos and discuss what reasons they represent. Then predict some other reasons the professor might mention.

The effects of drought in East Kenya

An unemployed man looking for work

WHILE LISTENING

LISTENING FOR
MAIN IDEAS
B   🎧 **Track 23**   ▶ **3.1**   Listen to the lecture. Check (✓) the statements that match points the professor makes.

1. _____ There are two kinds of migration: domestic and international.

2. _____ Push factors give people a reason to emigrate from a country.

3. _____ Pull factors make a country attractive to potential immigrants.

4. _____ Countries with strong economies rarely experience emigration.

5. _____ Push and pull factors can be divided into several categories.

6. _____ The majority of people who migrate can speak two languages.

NOTE-TAKING SKILL   Noting Contrasting Ideas

During lectures or presentations, it is common for speakers to contrast one idea with one or more other ideas. In some cases, the ideas may be different such as economic stability and political stability; in other cases, they may be opposite ideas such as immigration and emigration. When you hear speakers mention contrasting ideas, make a note of what they say. You can use a slash (/) to mark a contrast.

C 🔊 **Track 23** Listen again to the lecture. As you listen, complete these notes with words from the lecture. Write one word only in each blank.

NOTE TAKING

Migration can be:

- forced or _____
  1

- domestic or _____
  2

Emigration = out of a country

Immigration = into a country

Push factors – cause emigration

- economic / societal / _____
  3

_____ factors – attract immigration:
4

- also economic / societal / environmental

Exact reason(s) for migration typically _____ of push and pull factors;
5

(for both: _____ factors usually most important)
6

New migrants may face _____ barrier; discrimination
7

AFTER LISTENING

D Work with a partner. Think of a city, area, or country you would both be interested in migrating to. Which factors might influence your decision? Fill in the chart. Then share your ideas with the class. Which factors seem to be strongest?

PERSONALIZING

Where we would migrate to: _____		
	Push Factors	Pull Factors
Economic		
Societal		
Environmental		

A Speaking

A Interview two of your classmates. Write their answers in the blanks. When it is your turn to be interviewed, speak in full sentences.

1. What is a book you have read that was good enough to read at least twice?

   _____   _____

2. What is something you want that you don't have enough money to buy?

   _____   _____

3. What is one kind of food you love but think is too unhealthy to eat often?

   _____   _____

4. What is something you enjoy that you have too little time to do these days?

   _____   _____

5. What is one annoying thing you think too many people are doing these days?

   _____   _____

B Work with a partner you didn't interview in exercise A. Share what you learned about one of the people you interviewed.

> *One of the people I interviewed was Jung Ho. He said that …*

The Hundertwasser House, an apartment building in Vienna, Austria

C Work in a small group. Think about what makes a city a great place to live. Complete the sentences with different ideas. Then compare your answers with another group.

1. A city needs to have enough _____ .

2. Residents of a city should have enough _____ .

3. There shouldn't be too much _____ .

4. _____ shouldn't be too expensive.

5. The city shouldn't have too many _____ .

PRONUNCIATION Linking

🎧 **Track 24** In natural, fluent speech, speakers typically link certain sounds.

1. A consonant sound with a vowel sound:
   The magazine publishes a list of the most livable cities.

2. A consonant sound with the same consonant sound:
   This neighborhood has some cheap places to live.

3. A vowel sound with a vowel sound:
   High housing costs are often a barrier to owning a home.

The Peace Bridge, for pedestrians and bicyclists, crosses the Bow River in Calgary, Canada.

D 🎧 **Track 25** Read the information about livable cities. How do you think each sentence would be spoken with linked sounds? Mark the links between sounds. Then listen to confirm your answers. Practice saying the sentences.

> *The Economist* magazine publishes an annual list of cities with the best living conditions. These "World's Most Livable Cities" have many of the things that people want in a city. These things include access to health care, good or great transportation, and relatively cheap places to live. In recent years, Melbourne in Australia, Vienna in Austria, and Vancouver, Toronto, and Calgary in Canada have all been in the top five.

E Think about a city you know well. Make notes in answer to these questions.

- What is the city called and where is it?
- What does the city have enough of?
- What does the city have too much of?
- How livable do you think the city is?

CRITICAL THINKING:
EVALUATING

F Work in a small group. Summarize your ideas from exercise E. Then discuss what specific features make a city attractive and livable.

< *I like San Jose because it's big enough to have a good variety of things to do.*

LESSON TASK Discussing a Case Study

CRITICAL THINKING Categorizing Information

An important part of critical thinking is being able to put ideas or information into categories or groups. You might categorize cities according to how livable they are, to their size, or to their geographical location.

A Work with a partner. Read the case study. Then add notes to complete the chart.

Case Study

Lana, who is 30 years old, lives in Zagreb, the capital of Croatia. She studied architecture at university. However, there are too few jobs for architects in her country, which makes it hard for her to find work in her field. As a result, she currently works as a retail assistant in a store. She can only work part-time because she also has to spend time taking care of her parents, both of whom are in poor health. Lana has heard that there are not enough architects and other professionals in New Zealand. Lana's husband, who is a nurse, argues that he and Lana should emigrate there even though neither of them speaks English well.

Reasons to Stay	Reasons to Move	
	Push Factors	Pull Factors

EVERYDAY LANGUAGE   Asking for or Giving Reasons

Asking for reasons
Why do you say/think that?
What's your reason for saying that?

Giving reasons
Why do I say/think this? Well, …
My main reason is that ….

B Your teacher will assign you to one of the groups below. Work with your group members to follow the steps.

Group A – Lana should stay in Croatia
Group B – Lana should move to New Zealand

1. In your group, discuss the reasons that support your position.
2. Groups A and B debate whether Lana should stay or leave by taking turns to give their reasons.
3. Have a class vote to decide which team had the stronger argument.

Video

A photo of immigrants on a wall of the abandoned Ellis Island Hospital is part of an art installation by French artist JR.

What Ellis Island Means Today

BEFORE VIEWING

A Work with a partner. Match these words from the video to their definitions. Then use a dictionary to check your answers.

Word	Meaning
1. _____ ancestors (n)	a. (informal) brave or showing courage
2. _____ faith (n)	b. a person who lives in a particular place
3. _____ generation (n)	c. a strong belief that something is good or true
4. _____ gutsy (adj)	d. people who are about the same age
5. _____ liberty (n)	e. freedom to live the way you want
6. _____ resident (n)	f. family members who lived a long time ago

B In a small group, read this short history of Ellis Island. Then discuss the questions.

> Between 1892 and 1954, more than 12 million immigrants entered the United States through Ellis Island. After arrival, they were checked for health issues. They were also asked 29 interview questions, including some about the United States such as: What is the national anthem called? What are the three branches of government? Who was the first president? Who is the current president? What are the names of the 13 original colonies?

1. How many of the five questions can you answer? Where could you find the answers to the questions you don't know?
2. Do you think immigrants should be asked questions like these? Why or why not?

WHILE VIEWING

C ▶ 3.2 Watch the video. Which statement best summarizes the main message of the video?

UNDERSTANDING MAIN IDEAS

a. Many citizens of the United States currently live on Ellis Island.
b. Ellis Island is important in the family history of many Americans.
c. The Statue of Liberty is a symbol of the long history of Ellis Island.
d. Most immigrants on Ellis Island were concerned about their bags.

D ▶ 3.2 Watch the video again. Correct these details. You will hear somebody say the correct information and/or see it on the screen.

UNDERSTANDING DETAILS

1. David Luchsinger is the son of people who came through Ellis Island.

2. Just over 1.8 million bags were lost in the United States in 2012.

3. Judith Leavell's grandmother was 30 when she arrived at Ellis Island.

4. Peter Wong's grandparents emigrated to Ellis Island from Hong Kong.

5. Raea Hillebrant says her ancestors emigrated from Lithuania in 1940.

6. The maximum number of daily visitors to Ellis Island during the summer is about 18,000.

AFTER VIEWING

E In the video, we learned that immigrants to Ellis Island only brought one or two bags. If you were emigrating to another country and could only bring one suitcase, what would you put in it? Make a list, and then share your ideas with a partner.

PERSONALIZING

F Work in a small group. Complete the steps.

CRITICAL THINKING: CATEGORIZING

1. Brainstorm some of the emotions that immigrants to Ellis Island might have felt.
2. Sort your list of emotions into two categories: positive and negative.
3. Join with another group and share your lists.

Vocabulary

A 🎧 **Track 26** Read and listen to the reports. Then work with a partner and discuss the likely meaning of each word in **blue**.

1. The professor began her lecture with an **overview** of migration within the United States in the middle of the nineteenth century. She said that for much of that period, the midwest and western regions were seen as the **frontier**.

2. The speaker explained that these days, more and more people are choosing to **relocate** from rural to urban areas. These people believe they have the **prospect** of a better life in a city.

3. The architect described a new high-tech **habitat** designed for areas with dangerous climates. Its most important **aspect** is its weight. Although designed for two dozen people to live in comfortably, it weighs less than a car.

4. The presenter argued that in the future, humans might live elsewhere in the **solar** system such as on Mars or even Mercury, the closest planet to the sun. He said that humans might **colonize** other planets within the next few decades.

5. The engineer gave a talk on some of the dangers people would **encounter** if they were to move to another planet. Despite the risks, she was optimistic that new technologies would soon allow humans to **survive** on other planets.

B Complete each definition with one of the words in **blue** from exercise A.

1. _____ (n) the edge of explored and civilized land

2. _____ (v) to send people to another place to gain control of it

3. _____ (n) a general review or summary of a subject or topic

4. _____ (v) to move somewhere new

5. _____ (v) to unexpectedly find or experience something

6. _____ (v) to continue to live, especially under difficult conditions

7. _____ (n) a place in which an animal or plant usually lives; a home

8. _____ (n) the possibility of some future event happening

9. _____ (adj) relating to the sun

10. _____ (n) a specific feature or part of something

C Work with a different partner. Take turns answering these questions.

1. What is one movie that you enjoyed watching? Give a short overview of it.

2. Where would you like to relocate to? Why?

3. Think about one of your dreams for the future. What is the prospect that it will come true?

4. What is your favorite subject at school? Which aspect of it do you like most?

5. Think about a difficult situation you have encountered. How did you deal with it?

▸ A 1950s illustration for a science fiction story

D Fill in this chart with as many nouns as you know. Then use a dictionary to fill in words you don't know and to check the meanings of each word.

Verb	Noun(s)
colonize	(3)
encounter	(1)
relocate	(1)
survive	(2)

E 🎧 **Track 27** Complete this description with the correct form of words from exercise A. You will need to use three different forms of one word. Then listen to check your answers.

In his classic science fiction novel *Red Mars*, Kim Stanley Robinson tells the

tale of a human _____ on Mars. The story describes the initial
              1

struggle for _____ of a small number of people in an artificial
            2

_____ on the surface of Mars. The other two books in the trilogy, *Green*
        3

Mars and *Blue Mars*, focus on the challenges—physical, emotional, and even social—

that these people _____ as they live on the _____
                   4   5

of human civilization. They also tell how the _____ turn Mars into
                                              6

a planet suitable for human life and then _____ other places in our
                                          7

_____ system.
        8

F Work in a small group. Discuss how you feel about science fiction movies and books. Use some of the adjectives below, and give examples to support your views.

appealing	dramatic	fascinating	uninteresting
childish	entertaining	realistic	unlikely

A: *I'm not a fan of science fiction, to be honest. For me, it's … because …*
B: *I'm the opposite. I really find sci-fi to be … The reason is that …*

B Listening A Study Group Discussion

BEFORE LISTENING

A Work in a small group. You are going to listen to three students discussing a presentation assignment. Based on what you've studied so far in Lesson B, what do you think their presentation will be about? Which aspects of giving a presentation might they discuss?

WHILE LISTENING

LISTENING SKILL Listening for the Order of Events
The specific order of actions or events is often important. The order in which speakers discuss information is often the same as the order of actions or events. However, sometimes speakers may discuss information out of order. Speakers can give the order by using:

1. Sequence words
   First, … / Then …, / After that, … / Finally, …

2. Time adverbs and adverbial phrases
   Initially, … / At the same time, … / Until … / Eventually, … / At the end, …

3. Time prepositions or conjunctions
   Before … / After … / During … / While … / When …

4. Verbal phrases
   To start off with, … / Now moving on, … / To conclude, …

LISTENING FOR
ORDER OF EVENTS

B 🎧 **Track 28** Listen to three students discussing a presentation they are going to give. Number these topics in the order students discuss them.

a. _____ what information their talk should include

b. _____ what their presentation should be titled

c. _____ when and where they should next meet

d. _____ which of them should discuss which points

LISTENING FOR
DETAILS

C 🎧 **Track 28** Listen again to the conversation. Take notes on the decisions that the students make.

D 🎧 **Track 29** Complete this summary, using your notes from exercise C. Write no more than three words in each blank. Then listen to check your answers.

The students discuss a presentation they are going to give. First, they decide on

"Human Migration: _____" as the title of their presentation.
                               1

After that, they agree that their talk should include information about the various

_____ factors that might cause people to leave Earth. They
              2

also discuss the types of _____ that humans will need if
                                    3

they are going to live on other worlds and when emigration to such places might

happen. After that, the students decide that their talk should mention which

_____ are likely to want to leave Earth. Finally, they agree
              4

that their presentation should include information about which other places in the

_____ such as the moon or Mars humans might emigrate to.
              5

AFTER LISTENING

E Work in a small group. Discuss these questions.

CRITICAL THINKING: EVALUATING

1. Look back at your ideas for exercise A. Which of your predictions were true about the discussion?

2. Choose one of the ideas below that you think the three students should also include in their presentation. Explain the reasons for your choice.

   a. how much human colonization of other worlds is expected to cost
   b. what issues humans who emigrate to other worlds are likely to face
   c. which countries, groups, or organizations should colonize space first

Speaking

SPEAKING SKILL Expressing Probability

There are several ways you can express how probable or improbable a future event is.

probable

I am sure that I will graduate this year.
I will definitely graduate this year.
It's possible that I will graduate.
I may graduate.
It seems unlikely I will graduate.
I probably won't graduate.
There's no chance I will graduate.
I definitely won't graduate.

improbable

A For each question below, ask a student and record the answer. Then share what you learned with somebody you did not interview.

1. What is something that you think is certain to happen in the future?

_____ thinks _____.

2. What is something that you imagine will probably happen in the future?

_____ imagines _____.

3. What is something that you believe is unlikely to happen in the future?

_____ believes _____.

4. What is something that you feel will definitely not happen in the future?

_____ feels _____.

CRITICAL THINKING: CATEGORIZING

B Work with a partner. Brainstorm some reasons why people might want to emigrate from Earth to another planet. Fill in the T-chart to categorize each idea as either a push factor or a pull factor.

Push factors from Earth	Pull factors to a planet

C 🎧 **Track 30** Look at the infographic on the next page about SpaceX, a company that designs space transport. Add a phrase from the list below to complete each caption. Then listen to check your answers.

- 115 days
- $10 billion
- $100,000
- 75 pounds
- 200 people
- −80 degrees
- the year 2024
- 8 billion people

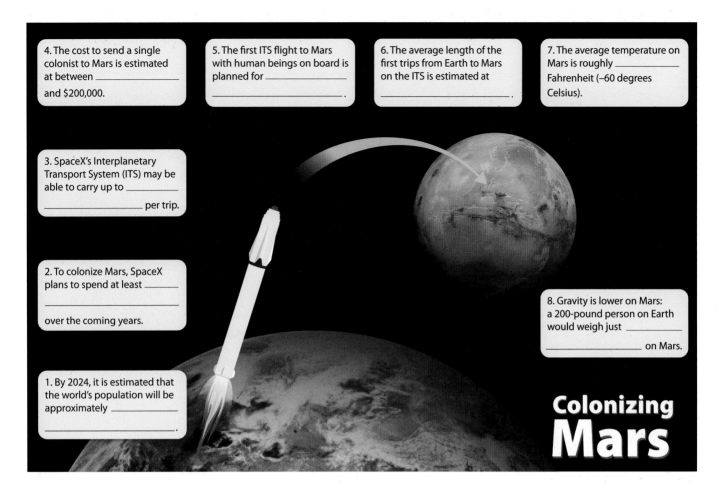

4. The cost to send a single colonist to Mars is estimated at between _____ and $200,000.

5. The first ITS flight to Mars with human beings on board is planned for _____ _____ .

6. The average length of the first trips from Earth to Mars on the ITS is estimated at _____ .

7. The average temperature on Mars is roughly _____ Fahrenheit (–60 degrees Celsius).

3. SpaceX's Interplanetary Transport System (ITS) may be able to carry up to _____ _____ per trip.

2. To colonize Mars, SpaceX plans to spend at least _____ _____ over the coming years.

8. Gravity is lower on Mars: a 200-pound person on Earth would weigh just _____ _____ on Mars.

1. By 2024, it is estimated that the world's population will be approximately _____ .

Colonizing Mars

D How likely is it that each of these things will happen? Discuss in a small group. Support your ideas with reasons and details.

- SpaceX will achieve its goal of colonizing Mars for less than the estimated budget.
- SpaceX will achieve its goal of sending a crewed mission to Mars before 2030.

E Work in a small group. What skills or knowledge will the first colonists on Mars need? Note your ideas under the correct category. Then share your ideas with another group.

CRITICAL THINKING: EVALUATING

A: *So, what do you think? What technical skills would colonists need?*
B: *I think being able to program computers would be vital, don't you?*
C: *Yeah, that's a good idea. And perhaps they'd need to be good at …*

Technical Skills	Personal Skills	Other Skills

FINAL TASK Presenting a Viewpoint

You and a partner are going to give a five-minute presentation about the colonization of Mars. Choose one of these viewpoints, or use your own. Then find a partner who has the same point of view:

- Humans should focus on colonizing Mars as soon as possible.
- Humans should fix the problems on Earth before colonizing Mars.
- Humans are meant to live on Earth; we should not colonize Mars.

PRESENTATION SKILL Expressing Your Opinion Strongly

If you want to express a strong opinion about something, you can use certain adverbs and adjectives to emphasize your words. Here are some examples of natural collocations:

I **really** think…   It is our **firm** belief that…

We **strongly** believe…   It is my **honest** feeling that…

I **definitely** feel…   It is our **strong** opinion that…

ORGANIZING IDEAS **A** Work with your partner. Complete these steps.

1. Decide what ideas, reasons, details, and examples you will use to support your point of view. Do some research if necessary.
2. Find images or visuals you could use to support your point of view.
3. Decide how to organize your talk and who will say what. Write an outline and notes.
4. Practice giving your presentation and finishing within the time limit.

PRESENTING **B** Work with another pair of students. Give your presentation. Listen to feedback from the other pair about how you could improve your talk. Then watch their presentation and give feedback to them.

REFLECTION

1. What is the most useful skill you learned in this unit? Explain.

   _____

   _____

2. What was the most interesting thing that you learned about human migration? Explain.

   _____

   _____

3. Here are the vocabulary words from the unit. Check (✓) the ones you can use.

   ☐ aspect AWL   ☐ frontier   ☐ relocate AWL
   ☐ barrier   ☐ habitat   ☐ settle
   ☐ colonize   ☐ immigration AWL   ☐ solar
   ☐ discrimination AWL   ☐ migrant AWL   ☐ stability AWL
   ☐ domestic AWL   ☐ nation   ☐ survive AWL
   ☐ emigration   ☐ overview   ☐ voluntary AWL
   ☐ encounter AWL   ☐ prospect AWL

Independent Student Handbook

Table of Contents

Listening Skills page 61
Note-Taking Skills page 63
Organizing Information page 64
Speaking: Common Phrases page 66
Speaking: Phrases for Presenting page 68
Presentation Strategies page 69
Presentation Outline page 71
Pronunciation Guide page 72
Vocabulary Building Strategies page 73

LISTENING SKILLS

Predicting

Speakers giving formal talks usually begin by introducing themselves and their topic. Listen carefully to the introduction of the topic so that you can predict what the talk will be about.

Strategies:

- Use visual information including titles on the board or on presentation slides.
- Think about what you already know about the topic.
- Ask yourself questions that you think the speaker might answer.
- Listen for specific phrases that indicate an introduction (e.g., *My topic is…*).

Listening for Main Ideas

It is important to be able to tell the difference between a speaker's main ideas and supporting details. It is more common for teachers to test understanding of main ideas than of specific details.

Strategies:

- Listen carefully to the introduction. Speakers often state the main idea in the introduction.
- Listen for rhetorical questions, or questions that the speaker asks, and then answers. Often the answer is the statement of the main idea.
- Notice words and phrases that the speaker repeats. Repetition often signals main ideas.

Listening for Details (Examples)

A speaker often provides examples that support a main idea. A good example can help you understand and remember the main idea better.

Strategies:

- Listen for specific phrases that introduce examples.
- Listen for general statements. Examples often follow general statements.

Listening for Details (Cause and Effect)

Speakers often give reasons or list causes and/or effects to support their ideas.

Strategies:

- Notice nouns that might signal causes/reasons (e.g., *factors, influences, causes, reasons*) or effects/results (e.g., *effects, results, outcomes, consequences*).
- Notice verbs that might signal causes/reasons (e.g., *contribute to, affect, influence, determine, produce, result in*) or effects/results (often these are passive, e.g., *is affected by*).

Understanding the Structure of a Presentation

An organized speaker uses expressions to alert the audience to important information that will follow. Recognizing signal words and phrases will help you understand how a presentation is organized and the relationship between ideas.

Introduction

A good introduction identifies the topic and gives an idea of how the lecture or presentation will be organized. Here are some expressions to introduce a topic:

I'll be talking about . . .   *My topic is . . .*

There are basically two groups . . .   *There are three reasons . . .*

Body

In the body of a lecture, speakers usually expand upon the topic. They often use phrases that signal the order of events or subtopics and their relationship to each other. Here are some expressions to help listeners follow the body of a lecture:

The first/next/final (point/reason) is . . .   *First/Next/Finally, let's look at . . .*

Another reason is . . .   *However, . . .*

Conclusion

In the conclusion of a lecture, speakers often summarize what they have said. They may also make predictions or suggestions. Sometimes they ask a question in the conclusion to get the audience to think more about the topic. Here are some expressions to give a conclusion:

In conclusion, . . .   *In summary, . . .*

As you can see. . .   *To review, + (restatement of main points)*

Understanding Meaning from Context

When you are not familiar with a word that a speaker says, you can sometimes guess the meaning of the word or fill in the gaps using the context or situation itself.

Strategies:

- Don't panic. You don't always understand every word of what a speaker says in your first language, either.
- Use context clues to fill in the blanks. What did you understand just before or just after the missing part? What did the speaker probably say?
- Listen for words and phrases that signal a definition or explanation (e.g., *What that means is…*).

Recognizing a Speaker's Bias

Speakers often have an opinion about the topic they are discussing. It's important for you to know if they are objective or subjective about the topic. Objective speakers do not express an opinion. Subjective speakers have a bias or a strong feeling about the topic.

Strategies:

- Notice words like adjectives, adverbs, and modals that the speaker uses (e.g., *ideal, horribly, should, shouldn't*). These suggest that the speaker has a bias.
- Listen to the speaker's voice. Does he or she sound excited, angry, or bored?
- Notice if the speaker gives more weight or attention to one point of view over another.
- Listen for words that signal opinions (e.g., *I think…*).

NOTE-TAKING SKILLS

Taking notes is a personalized skill. It is important to develop a note-taking system that works for you. However, there are some common strategies to improve your note taking.

Before You Listen

Focus

Try to clear your mind before the speaker begins so you can pay attention. If possible, review previous notes or think about what you already know about the topic.

Predict

If you know the topic of the talk, think about what you might hear.

Listen

Take Notes by Hand

Research suggests that taking notes by hand rather than on a computer is more effective. Taking notes by hand requires you to summarize, rephrase, and synthesize information. This helps you *encode* the information, or put it into a form that you can understand and remember.

Listen for Signal Words and Phrases

Speakers often use signal words and phrases (e.g., *Today we're going to talk about…*) to organize their ideas and show relationships between them. Listening for signal words and phrases can help you decide what information to write in your notes.

Condense (Shorten) Information

- As you listen, focus on the most important ideas. The speaker will usually repeat, define, explain, and/or give examples of these ideas. Take notes on these ideas.

  Speaker: *The Itaipu Dam provides about 20% of the electricity used in Brazil and about 75% of the electricity used in Paraguay. That electricity goes to millions of homes and businesses, so it's good for the economy of both countries.*

  Notes: Itaipu Dam → electricity: Brazil 20%, Paraguay 75%

- Don't write full sentences. Write only key words (nouns, verbs, adjectives, and adverbs), phrases, or short sentences.

  Full sentence: *Teachers are normally at the top of the list of happiest jobs.*

  Notes: teachers happiest

- Leave out information that is obvious.

    Full sentence: *Photographer Annie Griffiths is famous for her beautiful photographs. She travels all over the world to take photos.*

    Notes: A. *Griffiths famous for photos; travels world*

- Write numbers and statistics using numerals (9 bil; 35%).
- Use abbreviations (e.g., *ft., min., yr*) and symbols (=, ≠, >, <, %, →).
- Use indenting. Write main ideas on the left side of the paper. Indent details.

    Benefits of eating ugly foods
        Save $
            10-20% on ugly fruits & vegs. at market

- Write details under key terms to help you remember them.
- Write the definitions of important new words.

After You Listen

- Review your notes soon after the lecture or presentation. Add any details you missed.
- Clarify anything you don't understand in your notes with a classmate or teacher.
- Add or highlight main ideas. Cross out details that aren't important or necessary.
- Rewrite anything that is hard to read or understand. Rewrite your notes in an outline or other graphic organizer to organize the information more clearly.
- Use arrows, boxes, diagrams, or other visual cues to show relationships between ideas.

ORGANIZING INFORMATION

You can use a graphic organizer to take notes while you are listening, or to organize your notes after you listen. Here are some examples of graphic organizers:

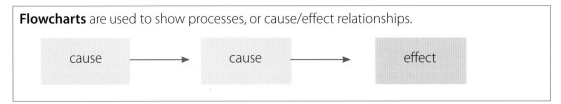

Flowcharts are used to show processes, or cause/effect relationships.

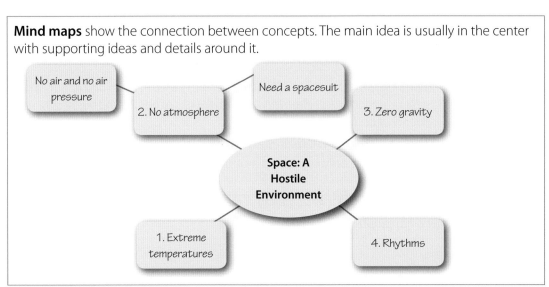

Mind maps show the connection between concepts. The main idea is usually in the center with supporting ideas and details around it.

Outlines show the relationship between main ideas and details.

To use an outline for taking notes, write the main ideas at the left margin of your paper. Below the main ideas, indent and write the supporting ideas and details. You may do this as you listen, or go back and rewrite your notes as an outline later.

> **I. Introduction:** How to feed the world
>
> **II. Steps**
>
>   Step One: Stop deforestation
>
>   a. stop burning rainforests
>
>   b. grow crops on land size of South America

T-charts compare two topics.

Climate Change in Greenland	
Benefits	**Drawbacks**
shorter winters	rising sea levels

Timelines show a sequence of events.

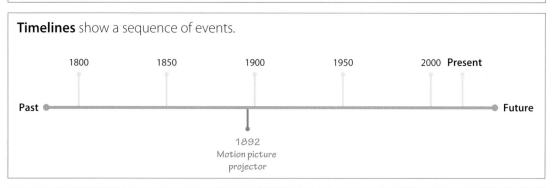

Venn diagrams compare and contrast two or more topics. The overlapping areas show similarities.

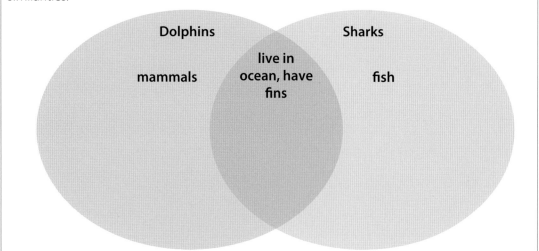

SPEAKING: COMMON PHRASES

Phrases for Expressing Yourself

Expressing Opinions	Expressing Likes and Dislikes
I think…	*I like…*
I believe…	*I prefer…*
I'm sure…	*I love…*
In my opinion/view…	*I can't stand…*
If you ask me,…	*I hate…*
Personally,…	*I really don't like…*
To me,…	*I don't care for…*

Giving Facts	Giving Tips or Suggestions
There is evidence/proof…	*Imperatives (e.g., Try to get more sleep.)*
Experts claim/argue…	*You/We should/shouldn't…*
Studies show…	*You/We ought to…*
Researchers found…	*It's (not) a good idea to…*
The record shows…	*I suggest (that)…*
	Let's…
	How about… + (noun/gerund)
	What about… + (noun/gerund)
	Why don't we/you…
	You/We could…

Agreeing	Disagreeing
I agree.	*I disagree.*
True.	*I'm not so sure about that.*
Good point.	*I don't know.*
Exactly.	*That's a good point, but I don't agree.*
Absolutely.	*I see what you mean, but I think that…*
I was just about to say that.	
Definitely.	
Right!	

Phrases for Interacting with Others

Clarifying/Checking Your Understanding

So are you saying that…?
So what you mean is…?
What do you mean?
How's that?
How so?
I'm not sure I understand/follow.
Do you mean…?
I'm not sure what you mean.

Asking for Clarification/Confirming Understanding

Sorry, I didn't catch that. Could you repeat it?
I'm not sure I understand the question.
I'm not sure I understand what you mean.
Sorry, I'm not following you.
Are you saying that…?
If I understand correctly, you're saying that…
Oh, now I get it. You're talking about…, right?

Checking Others' Understanding

Does that make sense?
Do you understand?
Do you see what I mean?
Is that clear?
Are you following/with me?
Do you have any questions?

Asking for Opinions

What do you think?
We haven't heard from you in a while.
Do you have anything to add?
What are your thoughts?
How do you feel?
What's your opinion?

Taking Turns

Can/May I say something?
Could I add something?
Can I just say…?
May I continue?
Can I finish what I was saying?
Did you finish your thought?
Let me finish.
Let's get back to…

Interrupting Politely

Excuse me.
Pardon me.
Forgive me for interrupting…
I hate to interrupt but…
Can I stop you for a second?

Asking for Repetition

Could you say that again?
I'm sorry?
I didn't catch what you said.
I'm sorry. I missed that. What did you say?
Could you repeat that please?

Showing Interest

I see.	*Good for you.*
Really?	*Seriously?*
Um-hmm.	*No kidding!*
Wow.	*And? (Then what?)*

That's funny / amazing / incredible / awful!

SPEAKING: PHRASES FOR PRESENTING

Introduction

Introducing a Topic

I'm going to talk about…
My topic is…
I'm going to present…
I plan to discuss…
Let's start with…

Today we're going to talk about…
So we're going to show you…
Now/Right/So/Well, (pause), let's look at…
There are three groups/reasons/effects/ factors…
There are four steps in this process.

Body

Listing or Sequencing

First/First of all/The first (noun)/To start/To begin,…
Second/Secondly/The second/Next/Another/ Also/Then/In addition,…
Last/The last/Finally,…
There are many/several/three types/kinds of/ ways…

Signaling Problems/Solutions

One problem/issue/challenge is…
One solution/answer/response is…

Giving Reasons or Causes

Because + (clause): Because the climate is changing…
Because of + (noun phrase): Because of climate change…
Due to + (noun phrase)…
Since + (clause)
The reason that I like hip-hop is…
One reason that people listen to music is…
One factor is + (noun phrase)
The main reason that…

Giving Results or Effects

so + (clause): so I went to the symphony
Therefore, + (sentence): Therefore, I went to the symphony.
As a result, + (sentence)
Consequently, + (sentence)
…causes + (noun phrase)
…leads to + (noun phrase)
…had an impact/effect on + (noun phrase)
If…then…

Giving Examples

The first example is…
Here's an example of what I mean…
For instance,…
For example,…
Let me give you an example…
…such as…
…like…

Repeating and Rephrasing

What you need to know is…
I'll say this again…
So again, let me repeat…
The most important point is…

Signaling Additional Examples or Ideas	Signaling to Stop Taking Notes
Not only…, but	*You don't need this for the test.*
Besides…	*This information is in your books/on your handout/on the website.*
Not only do…, but also	*You don't have to write all this down.*

Identifying a Side Track	Returning to a Previous Topic
This is off-topic,…	*Getting back to our previous discussion,…*
On a different subject,…	*To return to our earlier topic…*
As an aside, …	*OK, getting back on topic…*
That reminds me…	*So to return to what we were saying,…*

Signaling a Definition	Talking about Visuals
Which means…	*This graph/infographic/diagram shows/explains…*
What that means is…	*The line/box/image represents…*
Or…	*The main point of this visual is…*
In other words,…	*You can see…*
Another way to say that is…	*From this we can see…*
That is…	
That is to say…	

Conclusion

Concluding	
Well/So, that's how I see it.	*To sum up,*
In conclusion,	*As you can see,…*
In summary,	*At the end,…*
	To review, (+ restatement of main points)

PRESENTATION STRATEGIES

You will often have to give individual or group presentations in your class. The strategies below will help you to prepare, present, and reflect on your presentations.

Prepare

As you prepare your presentation:

Consider Your Topic

- **Choose a topic you feel passionate about.** If you are passionate about your topic, your audience will be more interested and excited about your topic, too. Focus on one major idea that you can bring to life. The best ideas are the ones your audience wants to experience.

Consider Your Purpose

- **Have a strong start.** Use an effective hook, such as a quote, an interesting example, a rhetorical question, or a powerful image to get your audience's attention. Include one sentence that explains what you will do in your presentation and why.
- **Stay focused.** Make sure your details and examples support your main points. Avoid sidetracks or unnecessary information that takes you away from your topic.
- **Use visuals that relate to your ideas.** Drawings, photos, video clips, infographics, charts, maps, slides, and physical objects can get your audience's attention and explain ideas effectively. For example, a photo or map of a location you mention can help your audience picture a place they have never been. Slides with only key words and phrases can help emphasize your main points. Visuals should be bright, clear, and simple.
- **Have a strong conclusion.** A strong conclusion should serve the same purpose as a strong start—to get your audience's attention and make them think. Good conclusions often refer back to the introduction, or beginning of the presentation. For example, if you ask a question in the beginning, you can answer it in the conclusion. Remember to restate your main points, and add a conclusion device such as a question, a call to action, or a quote.

Consider Your Audience

- **Use familiar concepts.** Think about the people in your audience. Ask yourself these questions: Where are they from? How old are they? What is their background? What do they already know about my topic? What information do I need to explain? Use language and concepts they will understand.
- **Share a personal story.** Consider presenting information that will get an emotional reaction; for example, information that will make your audience feel surprised, curious, worried, or upset. This will help your audience relate to you and your topic.
- **Be authentic (be yourself!).** Write your presentation yourself. Use words that you know and are comfortable using.

Rehearse

- **Make an outline** to help you organize your ideas.
- **Write notes on notecards.** Do not write full sentences, just key words and phrases to help you remember important ideas. Mark the words you should stress and places to pause.
- **Review pronunciation.** Check the pronunciation of words you are uncertain about with a classmate, a teacher, or in a dictionary. Note and practice the pronunciation of difficult words.
- **Memorize the introduction and conclusion.** Rehearse your presentation several times. Practice saying it out loud to yourself (perhaps in front of a mirror or video recorder) and in front of others.
- **Ask for feedback.** Note and revise information that doesn't flow smoothly based on feedback and on your own performance in rehearsal. If specific words or phrases are still a problem, rephrase them.

Present

As you present:

- **Pay attention to your pacing** (how fast or slow you speak). Remember to speak slowly and clearly. Pause to allow your audience to process information.
- **Speak at a volume loud enough to be heard** by everyone in the audience, but not too loud. Ask the audience if your volume is OK at the beginning of your talk.

- **Vary your intonation.** Don't speak in the same tone throughout the talk. Your audience will be more interested if your voice rises and falls, speeds up and slows down to match the ideas you are talking about.
- **Be friendly and relaxed with your audience**—remember to smile!
- **Show enthusiasm for your topic.** Use humor if appropriate.
- **Have a relaxed body posture.** Don't stand with your arms folded, or look down at your notes. Use gestures when helpful to emphasize your points.
- **Don't read directly from your notes.** Use them to help you remember ideas.
- **Don't look at or read from your visuals too much.** Use them to support your ideas.
- **Make frequent eye contact** with the entire audience.

Reflect

As you reflect on your presentation:

- **Consider what you think went well** during your presentation and what areas you can improve upon.
- **Get feedback** from your classmates and teacher. How do their comments relate to your own thoughts about your presentation? Did they notice things you didn't? How can you use their feedback in your next presentation?

PRESENTATION OUTLINE

When you are planning a presentation, you may find it helpful to use an outline. If it is a group presentation, the outline can provide an easy way to divide the content. For example, one student can do the introduction, another student the first idea in the body, and so on.

1. Introduction

Topic: _____

Hook: _____

Statement of main idea: _____

2. Body

First step/example/reason: _____

    Supporting details: _____ _____ _____

Second step/example/reason: _____

    Supporting details: _____ _____ _____

Third step/example/reason: _____

    Supporting details: _____ _____ _____

3. Conclusion

Main points to summarize: _____ _____

Suggestions/Predictions: _____ _____

Closing comments/summary: _____ _____

PRONUNCIATION GUIDE

Sounds and Symbols

Vowels

Symbol	Key Words
/ɑ/	hot, stop
/æ/	cat, ran
/aɪ/	fine, nice
/i/	eat, need
/ɪ/	sit, him
/eɪ/	name, say
/ɛ/	get, bed
/ʌ/	cup, what
/ə/	about, lesson
/u/	boot, new
/ʊ/	book, could
/oʊ/	go, road
/ɔ/	law, walk
/aʊ/	house, now
/ɔɪ/	toy, coin

Consonants

Symbol	Key Word	Symbol	Key Word
/b/	boy	/t/	tea
/d/	day	/tʃ/	cheap
/dʒ/	job, bridge	/v/	vote
/f/	face	/w/	we
/g/	go	/y/	yes
/h/	hat	/z/	zoo
/k/	key, car		
/l/	love	/ð/	they
/m/	my	/θ/	think
/n/	nine	/ʃ/	shoe
/ŋ/	sing	/ʒ/	measure
/p/	pen		
/r/	right		
/s/	see		

Source: *The Newbury House Dictionary plus Grammar Reference,* Fifth Edition, National Geographic Learning/ Cengage Learning, 2014.

Rhythm

The rhythm of English involves stress and pausing.

Stress

- English words are based on syllables—units of sound that include one vowel sound.

- In every word in English, one syllable has the primary stress.

- In English, speakers group words that go together based on the meaning and context of the sentence. These groups of words are called *thought groups*. In each thought group, one word is stressed more than the others—the stress is placed on the syllable with the primary stress in this word.

- In general, new ideas and information are stressed.

Pausing

- Pauses in English can be divided into two groups: long and short pauses.

- English speakers use long pauses to mark the conclusion of a thought, items in a list, or choices given.

- Short pauses are used in between thought groups to break up the ideas in sentences into smaller, more manageable chunks of information.

English speakers use intonation, or pitch (the rise and fall of their voice), to help express meaning. For example, speakers usually use a rising intonation at the end of *yes/no* questions, and a falling intonation at the end of *wh-* questions and statements.

VOCABULARY BUILDING STRATEGIES

Vocabulary learning is an on-going process. The strategies below will help you learn and remember new vocabulary words.

Guessing Meaning from Context

You can often guess the meaning of an unfamiliar word by looking at or listening to the words and sentences around it. Speakers usually know when a word is unfamiliar to the audience, or is essential to understanding the main ideas, and often provide clues to its meaning.

- Repetition: A speaker may use the same key word or phrase, or use another form of the same word.
- Restatement or synonym: A speaker may give a synonym to explain the meaning of a word, using phrases such as *in other words, also called, or…, also known as.*
- Antonyms: A speaker may define a word by explaining what it is NOT. The speaker may say *Unlike A/In contrast to A, B is…*
- Definition: Listen for signals such as *which means* or *is defined as*. Definitions can also be signaled by a pause.
- Examples: A speaker may provide examples that can help you figure out what something is. For example, ***Mascots*** *are a very popular marketing tool. You've seen them on commercials and in ads on social media –* ***cute, brightly colored creatures that help sell a product***.

Understanding Word Families: Stems, Prefixes, and Suffixes

Use your understanding of stems, prefixes, and suffixes to recognize unfamiliar words and to expand your vocabulary. The stem is the root part of the word, which provides the main meaning. A prefix comes before the stem and usually modifies meaning (e.g., adding *re-* to a word means "again" or "back"). A suffix comes after the stem and usually changes the part of speech (e.g., adding *-ion, -tion,* or *-ation* to a verb changes it to a noun). Words that share the same stem or root belong to the same word family (e.g., *event, eventful, uneventful, uneventfully*).

Word Stem	Meaning	Example
ann, enn	year	anniversary, millennium
chron(o)	time	chronological, synchronize
flex, flect	bend	flexible, reflection
graph	draw, write	graphics, paragraph
lab	work	labor, collaborate
mob, mot, mov	move	automobile, motivate, mover
port	carry	transport, import
sect	cut	sector, bisect

Prefix	Meaning	Example
dis-	not, opposite of	disappear, disadvantages
in-, im-, il-, ir-	not	inconsistent, immature, illegal, irresponsible
inter-	between	Internet, international
mis-	bad, badly, incorrectly	misunderstand, misjudge
pre-	before	prehistoric, preheat
re-	again; back	repeat; return
trans-	across, beyond	transfer, translate
un-	not	uncooked, unfair

Suffix	Meaning	Example
-able, -ible	worth, ability	believable, impossible
-en	to cause to become; made of	lengthen, strengthen; golden
-er, -or	one who	teacher, director
-ful	full of	beautiful, successful
-ify, -fy	to make or become	simplify, satisfy
-ion, -tion, -ation	condition, action	occasion, education, foundation
-ize	cause	modernize, summarize
-ly	in the manner of	carefully, happily
-ment	condition or result	assignment, statement
-ness	state of being	happiness, sadness

Using a Dictionary

Here are some tips for using a dictionary:

- When you see or hear a new word, try to guess its part of speech (noun, verb, adjective, etc.) and meaning, then look it up in a dictionary.
- Some words have multiple meanings. Look up a new word in the dictionary and try to choose the correct meaning for the context. Then see if it makes sense within the context.
- When you look up a word, look at all the definitions to see if there is a basic core meaning. This will help you understand the word when it is used in a different context. Also look at all the related words, or words in the same family. This can help you expand your vocabulary. For example, the core meaning of *structure* involves something built or put together.

> **structure** /ˈstrʌktʃər/ *n.* **1** [C] a building of any kind: *A new structure is being built on the corner.* **2** [C] any architectural object of any kind: *The Eiffel Tower is a famous Parisian structure.* **3** [U] the way parts are put together or organized: *the structure of a song‖a business's structure*
> *–v.* [T] **-tured, -turing, -tures** to put together or organize parts of s.t.: *We are structuring a plan to hire new teachers.*
> *-adj.* **structural.**

Source: *The Newbury House Dictionary plus Grammar Reference*, Fifth Edition, National Geographic Learning/Cengage Learning, 2014

Multi-Word Units

You can improve your fluency if you learn and use vocabulary as multi-word units: idioms (*go the extra mile*), collocations (*wide range*), and fixed expressions (*in other words*). Some multi-word units can only be understood as a chunk—the individual words do not add up to the same overall meaning. Keep track of multi-word units in a notebook or on notecards.

Vocabulary Note Cards

You can expand your vocabulary by using vocabulary note cards or a vocabulary building app. Write the word, expression, or sentence that you want to learn on one side. On the other, draw a four-square grid and write the following information in the squares: definition; translation (in your first language); sample sentence; synonyms. Choose words that are high frequency or on the academic word list. If you have looked a word up a few times, you should make a card for it.

definition:	first language translation:
sample sentence:	synonyms:

Organize the cards in review sets so you can practice them. Don't put words that are similar in spelling or meaning in the same review set as you may get them mixed up. Go through the cards and test yourself on the words or expressions. You can also practice with a partner.

VOCABULARY INDEX

Word	Page	CEFR† Level	Word	Page	CEFR† Level	Word	Page	CEFR† Level
addictive	4	C1	factor*	24	B2	purchase*	4	B2
alter*	4	B1	findings	14	off list	relocate*	54	C1
aspect*	54	B2	frontier	54	C2	reproduce	24	C2
assume*	4	B2	frustrating	14	C1	resemble	34	C1
bargain	4	B2	gender*	14	B2	responsibility	24	B2
barrier	44	B2	habitat	54	C1	retail	4	C1
challenge*	24	B1	immigration*	44	B1	settle	44	B2
chore	14	C1	interact*	14	B2	shelter	34	B2
colonize/colonise	54	off list	loyalty	14	B2	solar	54	B2
colony	24	off list	manufacture	34	B2	specialize/specialise	34	B2
commercial	4	B2	method*	34	B1	stability*	44	C1
complex*	4	B2	migrant*	44	off list	struggle	24	B2
conduct*	14	B2	mission	14	B2	substance	34	B2
consume*	34	B2	nation	44	B2	sufficient*	14	B2
consumer*	4	B2	organism	34	off list	survive*	54	B2
discrimination*	44	C1	out of stock	14	B2	territory	24	B2
domestic*	44	B2	overview	54	C1	threaten	24	B2
emigration	44	off list	predators	24	C1	transfer*	34	B1
encounter*	54	B2	primary*	34	B2	voluntary*	44	C1
extinction	24	C1	prospect*	54	B2			

†The Common European Framework of Reference for Languages (CEFR) is an international standard for describing language proficiency.

*These words are on the Academic Word List (AWL). The AWL is a list of the 570 highest-frequency academic word families that regularly appear in academic texts. The AWL was compiled by researcher Averil Coxhead based on her analysis of a 3.5-million-word corpus (Coxhead, 2000).

NOTES

NOTES

NOTES

NOTES

NOTES

NOTES